THEY DON'T HAVE TO SEE YOU

BE A BETTER REMOTE MANAGER AND BUILD TRUST WITH YOUR EMPLOYEES

HOLLIS AVERY

To Anthony
Who has supported me, over and over.
And saved me, again and again.
I love you to the moon and back.

CONTENTS

INTRODUCTION

To improve is to change; to be perfect is to change often.
–Winston Churchill

In a world where technology makes lives easier, it can, at times, complicate some norms. The COVID-19 pandemic has transformed the working culture and the way each individual approaches their life ahead. The time off during lockdown has propelled many to reassess their current lifestyle and their careers. On the other hand, it spurred people to understand the freedom and flexibility of remote working. Soon, many understood that they could do their primary function in the comfort of their homes rather than commute, hustle at the office, and go home fully drained of energy. As a result, employees have led the remote working revolution that has left many managers unable to fulfill their objectives.

I had sleepless nights before. I woke up at 3 a.m. most nights and stared at my laptop in the kitchen. I didn't wake up to work during that time, but I was there pondering every second how I could get the best out of my team. We were a dispersed group— with different time zones from all over the world—finding our way to our goal with asynchronous communication. The pressure as a manager is huge, being held responsible for the success or failure of a team. I wanted to strive toward the former and get the best out of my remote team in this current situation. I probably had more sleepless nights and less time to spend with my family in this remote setup than I did when I managed teams on site. But soon I realized it was all in my head, and it was all about adapting to the current climate. Hence why I've started this journey to share with you how to manage your team remotely and efficiently while enjoying the flexibility it offers and fulfilling your organizational goals.

THE NEW AGE

The recent pandemic has affected many businesses and their working culture. It has forced companies to furlough employees, shut down their business, and take out more debts. Furthermore, it drove most employees to quit their current job to pursue their passionate side hustles or look for more flexibility. As a result, it was seen that more than 25% of the employed workforce were required to switch occupations just to stay valid in the market. Most businesses have adopted the remote working culture as they learned it can maximize productivity of employees and can reduce excessive administrative expenses. The employees relish the flexibility and most of them don't see themselves going back to working in an office again. However, the affected people have been the managers, who've been suffering from lack of communication from their remote team, and thus unable to get the best out of them.

"We as a business are very much office-first... I believe we can be a
stronger workforce when based in the office full time."
–James Rogers (a digital public relations lead manager in a British-
American global content agency)

James Rogers isn't the only one who feels that way. Over 70%
of current remote managers prefer to have employees back in the
office. That's a staggering number, and this proves that you are not
alone. Most managers do face challenges, such as having the lack
of control over their remote workers and being unsure if they are
performing their tasks or not. Lack of communication and transparency was seen as one of the other biggest challengers for
remote managers to lead a team effectively. Moreover, the lack of
face-to-face interaction and physical proximity has diminished
sentiments and made it easier for managers to turnover employees
and find difficulties in recruiting the right talent remotely. The
"new normal" has been difficult to cope with, and this leaves many
managers frustrated and confused over their future in
management.

HOW THIS BOOK CAN HELP YOU

Looking at the likely trend of the remote working culture, it is definitely here to stay, and it is up to you and many remote managers
out there to adapt to the new norm. It won't be easy, but no one
said it would be difficult. I can relate to your worries because I've
faced the same—the lack of human element in the remote work
setup has driven mistrust over my employees, the delayed communication wastes more time than ever, and the less tech-savvy
clients and employees encounter more problems that delay the
entire workflow. On top of that, it has proved difficult to assess an
individual's performance and work integrity in this setup. Ultimately, all this leads to more pressure on the managers.

Being a business coach and entrepreneur, I'm quite passionate about teaching more and more people how to optimize mainly the use of their human resources because I overcame that challenge and want to share with you a system that will put all your worries behind you. This book offers practical and doable strategies that will enable you to instill a positive remote working culture. Notice that I mentioned the word 'culture' because that's why most managers are failing to adapt to the current climate. The technology has given you a different way of doing things, and it is up to you to build a remote working culture that your team gets, and as a result, ensures you and your team will combine their efforts toward reaching those organizational goals.

This book is structured in a linear way, starting from building the foundations. It helps you to first establish a working model strategy, instill a working culture, show you ways to onboard talent effectively, make communication transparent, manage egos in your remote team, build strong relationships with your employees, and, moreover, the essentials to virtual team building. You will know what virtual tools and strategies you need to use to find solutions in each remote work process you encounter on a day-to-day basis. Once you have learned the essentials, this book can be used as your handy reference manual to look back at and help you in your daily operations. If you are ready to walk down the road to be a successful remote manager, then let's get started.

THE NEW WORLD ORDER

Working remotely and giving that extra flexibility to the workforce hasn't been the favorite way of working for many companies and was regularly criticized in the past. But with the 2020 pandemic, things changed on a global scale, giving rise to new working trends that most have to bow down to. Read on to find out more about the remote work culture, where it stands today, and how it is going to be in the future.

REMOTE CULTURE: AN INTRODUCTION

Remote work existed before the 2020 pandemic. However, the pandemic encouraged companies to take up remote work policy initially to not spread novel coronavirus between employees. But every cloud has a silver lining, and the nature of remote work has impacted employee performance and company overhead costs positively, so much so that many businesses prefer to keep this remote work policy indefinitely. Leveraging the digital tools on offer today, many have found comfort and the ability to maximize their productivity and earning potential through remote working. When you think about it, it all makes sense. Working remotely allows flexibility, eliminates all that time lost commuting from one place to another, and enables freedom for employees to take on multiple projects to maximize their revenue.

The Feel of Working Remotely

In the past, working remotely would have been a hassle due to lack of internet infrastructure and technology advancement. However, in an era where collaborative tools like Slack, Zoom, Skype, etc. have helped individuals to work from any part of the globe. Working remotely doesn't limit me to working from home alone. The remote culture goes well with "digital nomads" who take advantage of remote working and travel the world at the time. They travel the world and make sure they do their work from any location. This includes coffee shops, airports, hotels, malls, beaches, and many more comfort zones you can find to sit down and fully focus on your work. Nevertheless, it is crucial to keep in mind that not many job functions can cater to remote working. Occupations like doctors, construction workers, and other professions that require a high degree of physical proximity require being there physically having contact with customers. The most common professions that cater to remote work lifestyles are engineers, accountants, IT professionals, writers, consultants, tutors/teachers, etc.

Types of Remote Work

Anyone can work remotely and there are three major types of remote work set up you will need to know about. The first one is a full-time remote set up—where employees can work remotely at the comfort of their homes or any work location they choose, and do not require them to come to the main office. Back in 2020, Twitter announced that they will provide employees an option to work from home forever if it means their primary job function doesn't require them to come to the office. Companies that go fully remote gets an opportunity to recruit on a global scale and create job opportunities for foreign nationalities. Many companies have decided to go for 100% remote teams to lower overhead costs and this has offered employees greater flexibility and freedom during the day.

The second type of remote work is called hybrid. This phenomenon allows employees to work remotely for some days and on other days, they can come to the office. The hybrid options goes well with many individuals who need to have flexible time to take care of their children, spend more time with their family, which wouldn't be possible if they worked full-time commuting to a physical office. Following a hybrid model has been found to improve the workforce's mental health significantly because they are able to gain flexibility and spend time with their family at home, and come to the office often and socially engage with their peers. As a result, this balanced lifestyle has become popular with many who want to attain that ideal work-life balance.

The third type of remote work are not employees but free-lancers. Employees are associated with one company and they get additional benefits such as a base salary, health coverage, sick leaves, accommodation, 401k retirement plans, etc. Whereas free-lancers are independent contractors that can work contractually with multiple companies and get paid per project basis. A free-lancer has the freedom to work remotely or on site with the company, depending on the project. Unlike regular employees, they do not get other benefits and are thus responsible for their income and expenses.

Companies View on Remote Work Culture

Remote work can provide many options. For businesses, they can recruit employees and freelancers within the location they're based in or in that country, so they can work with clients in those locations. Some companies operate remotely during specific core business hours to give support to clients. However, there are mixed reactions in the corporate world towards the remote work culture. For instance, companies like Facebook and Twitter are showing interest in evolving their business to go remote forever while many other companies condemn this work culture. This is where the debate unfolds on why managers are left frustrated in their team's productivity when working remotely. Nonetheless, companies still find to make good use of remote work culture to achieve business goals and reduce work process time and overhead costs. It depends on the nature of work and how companies can maximize their resources in this digital era.

REMOTE CULTURE: THE EVOLUTION

When you think about the industrial revolution and the traditional regime of going to work from your home in the morning and coming back home at night, remote work culture was never going to sit right with most idealists. The remote way was often judged as "unproductive" or "lazy", mostly to do with the lack of supervision and control the manager would have over their employees. But with the recent pandemic and technological development, employers are slowly changing their viewpoint on it.

How It Has Evolved

Many decades ago, remote work was never in the minds of

employees or the employers. Except for telemarketers and telecommunication support, employees were used to the norm of working at their office desk or other job sites for several hours and going back home when the sun sets. Back then, employees didn't have smartphones and had to use a pager or a fax machine to communicate with other organizations and themselves.

Now, with the rise of technological options, many professions can make use of digital tools to efficiently achieve their tasks. Salesmen make use of video-conferencing tools like Zoom to meet prospects and close sales remotely. UI/UX Designers utilize collaborative tools like Figma online to design prototypes and share with their team in real-time. Cloud has been a robust central database for organizations to store and share unlimited files without the fear of losing them. As a result, organizations have slowly moved away from the traditional regime of working in offices or co-working spaces and opted to work remotely.

Furthermore, minimizing expenses on office rent, administrative costs, and other miscellaneous expenses have helped businesses increase their profit margin more than ever before. The internet has provided a platform for individuals to start businesses with lower investment and conduct them more efficiently than the traditional route of setting up a physical entity with much higher starting capital.

The Present Scenario

In the present day, businesses have adopted variations of fully remote and hybrid teams to achieve their goals. The remote work culture has created job opportunities for freelancers and employees living abroad to work with individual businesses with ease. Despite having many digital options, many companies are still not bought into the idea of going fully remote. As mentioned earlier in the previous section, it is mostly to do with the fear of employees' lack of productivity that could inhibit them from achieving organizational goals. Hence, companies implement a remote work policy of having to work a few days a week remotely, and some days in the office. Assessing the productivity levels in both has provided statistical results in the favor of remote workers over office-based workers.

According to a survey conducted by Airtasker, it was found that remote employees worked additional days per month despite taking longer breaks, were less distracted from their bosses, and were less unproductive compared to office-based employees. The myth that had hung around that working remotely would be unproductive was challenged by convincing statistical results. However, working remotely should be implemented the right way to maximize productivity and create less of those distractions. In most cases, remote workers have struggled to switch on and off between tasks whenever they work from home—their personal family life and work life ruining the flow of their typical day.

The Future Expectations

With Artificial Intelligence (AI) and machine learning at the helm, remote work is here to stay. There will be a point where organizations will rely on VR conferencing and other video-conferencing collaborative tools over physical meetings. Now, a point has been reached where companies cannot oppose the remote work revolution. Employees have already made their thoughts clear on the fact that remote work offers them better work/life balance and they are more accustomed to looking for remote-based jobs than regular office-based jobs.

In fact, remote employees would go as far as to take a small pay cut just to make sure they get the privilege to work remotely and spend time with their family. The trend won't fade away, and hence why businesses are looking to strategize their work-from-home or remote work policies to get the best out of their employees and have a proper IT infrastructure around them to support this smooth transition.

REMOTE CULTURE: A BLISS OR A BURDEN?

Now, let's understand whether the remote work lifestyle is a blessing or a big burden for businesses. This is quite debatable depending on the type of business and the nature of work you do. However, there are definitely some pros and cons to the remote work culture that has encouraged employees to opt to work from home more and discouraged employers from allowing their employees to work fully remote. Let us explore these benefits and the drawbacks of the remote lifestyle.

Flexibility and Enhanced Productivity

Without an ounce of doubt, the biggest plus point remote workers enjoy experiencing is the flexibility it offers. The ability to create your personal schedule and ensure the work gets done by the end of the day is a privilege many in the past would have loved having. As a result, employees can manage their time wisely, work a few hours during the morning, take a break during the afternoons, and work throughout the evenings if they opt for that. The flexibility has given employees more freedom to manage their work schedule as they can focus on deep work—which is crucial for more technical and creative work—for a few hours in a distraction-free environment, and utilize their energy later on for other tasks such as meetings and administrative tasks. In between that, they can choose to have a few hours of rest when they feel exhausted, which wouldn't have been possible in the traditional regime of calling in sick to work the day before.

As for the productivity side, it is often argued that when employees work remotely by themselves, it could leave them more distracted with personal matters and lower their productivity. However, this may not be a surprise to you, but it actually maximized their productivity even more because... think about it. They get to convert their energy efficiently for specific tasks in their preferred time slot. Additionally, rest is considered as being productive. Being remote has given them the luxury to take longer breaks and sleep well without the worry of commuting to offices far away, and refilling their energy tank has helped them to deliver better work quality and maximize their productivity to a greater extent.

Decreased Costs

Another plus point of the remote work lifestyle is that it takes the minimalistic approach and removes all the cluttered costs that complicates a typical work day. When it concerns employees, they are saving day-to-day travel expenses from home to work. Additionally, they are cutting down more costs on eating out during workdays. In the comfort of their own homes, they are able to find time and cook home-based meals that contribute to better health and lifestyle. Also, I believe there's less stress in managing our laundry of work clothes when working remotely than we would daily when commuting to the office. Don't you think?

As for the employers, this is a big benefit, too, concerning their total overhead costs. Remote means employees don't require office space, and they can remove those office expenses from their monthly expense chart for good. Affording rent, along with the utilities and administrative costs, can eat up those profit margins for companies. If they feel their job function can be performed virtually without the need for physical space, then this will be the first thing on their mind to reduce. They can save up all those equipment costs because the employees will have their personal setup at home to work with. That's a few thousand bucks saved right there for starters.

A Wide Talent Pool

With the rise of remote-based jobs, employees are continually on the lookout and prioritizing landing remote-based jobs over regular office-based jobs. This has led companies to transition themselves into a remote work friendly business and offer remote work as a necessity rather than an option. But the even better news for employers and employees is that it has opened up a world to hire anyone around the globe and be inclusive. Remote-based jobs create better career opportunities for people who are unable to commute to the desired location and help to access a more multi-cultural and talented candidate pool for hiring companies. The remote flexibility allows employees from different time zones to work on their own schedule and reach many clients across various countries in less time. Compare that to traditional times when meeting clients abroad and doing business took time and money, but now all you have to do is arrange a Zoom meeting and you're good to meet them online instantly.

Lack of Human Connection

On the flip side, remote-based work has some drawbacks to its uniqueness. One of them is the lack of human touch to the work that gets done on a daily basis. When you think of different situations, this will make more sense. When meeting with clients through video conferencing platforms, it doesn't offer room to improve interpersonal relationships with them. When you meet clients face-to-face and talk about business over dinner, it creates a better trust to do future business than the lack of human connection online. Another example is the lack of guidance for employees, especially when they are new to a job. When many employees are virtually onboarded, they will be left alone to settle in slowly in the company with the digital resources they have in hand. The lack of coaching and mentorship makes usual work processes tough to comprehend and discourages them from staying with the company longer.

On a side note, the lack of face-to-face interaction with employees has left employers with uncertainty regarding whether their employees are doing their work or not. The lack of supervision has made it difficult for managers to assess employee performance critically, and this makes it difficult to manage their team overall. Sometimes as humans, all we need is guidance and support to get through daily operations, and when it comes to the remote work lifestyle, it offers a minimum of that.

Decreased Coordination

Despite the number of collaborative tools in offer, remote coordination is not that effective compared to physically being there and working together. The asynchronous nature of collaborative tools makes it difficult for teams to work together in real-time and combine their efforts to achieve organizational success. Even though informality and those regular coffee or lunch breaks employees have together are not mandatory, it does make a significant impact on team coordination and ethos. If you look at the current remote work lifestyle, employees are more drawn to work individually than collectively because the remote lifestyle favors their individual productivity over their collaborative productivity. Just think of a specific project each time it is managed remotely—a sales team getting an inquiry, the assistant scheduling an appointment, the consultant virtually meeting the client, the specifications transferred to the technical team, the final delivery of business solution to the client—it can involve some delayed communication in between to ensure there's a smooth flow of coordination to complete a project.

Isolation

Speaking about those regular coffee and lunch breaks employees have together, the remote lifestyle has removed that tradition employees enjoy very much. The lack of human interaction and togetherness has left many employees isolated and feeling lonely when doing their work. The small chit-chats and giggles in a workplace do bond a team well, and they end up coordinating better. The difficulty of building a team can be seen in a remote setup. To combat this, it is wise to set up regular virtual meetings so employees can bond better regularly and have a feeling of togetherness that the remote work setup won't allow.

END OF CHAPTER REVIEW

- The remote culture has evolved during recent years. From the years of using pagers and fax machines, employees can now collaborate instantly using digital tools online.
- Even though some companies like Facebook and Twitter are looking to work remotely indefinitely, other companies are still skeptical of whether remote work can maximize an employee's productivity.
- With AI and machine learning, remote culture is here to stay, and it will soon become a necessity in many jobs rather than an option.

- Remote work offers employees work flexibility and freedom, reduces business and miscellaneous costs, and offers a wider talent pool for onboarding new employees.
- On the flip side, remote work minimizes human interaction, reduces team coordination, and, in some cases, leads to employee isolation.

2

TAKING THE REMOTE INTO YOUR HANDS

I f you ever wondered why the most successful businesses keep flourishing and the unsuccessful ones fade away, it is because they have a strong spine or backbone that cements their position in the market. A backbone refers to a business's system or working model that helps run day-to-day operations smoothly and makes it clear to everyone in the organization what is expected from them.

Most traditional businesses flourish with a strong backbone, but now times have changed as companies have transitioned to a remote work lifestyle. The remote working culture is quite new and hence requires a new approach toward managing the work-force. Read on to find out how you can create a healthy working space in the remote ecosystem.

CREATING THE REMOTE ECOSYSTEM

When it comes to traditional businesses, employees collaborate organically and combine their efforts to produce results daily. With a remote setup, without a shadow of a doubt, you will require more effort and intricate planning to get the best out of your team.

The disadvantage is shown right in front of your very eyes—the lack of real-time communication, supervision, assessment, and the technological complications that come with it. But what if I told you the solution is a lot simpler than you think? The best remote teams don't flourish by punching above their weight daily till they eventually burn out. They stay disciplined and motivated to carry out their duties because of one major factor—culture!

The Right Culture Matters

When you think about why sports teams have a togetherness and exhibit passion when performing as a team, it is mainly due to the culture within their camp. The continuous interaction between players, the effective rituals and training regimes, and a coach—that symbolizes a leader—guiding them through the highs and lows in a season; all these factors determine a culture within a team, and the same reasoning can be applied to businesses. Most businesses do practice nurturing the right culture, and it may seem a lot easier when doing it face-to-face.

But the real challenge begins when remote teams have to form a culture within their own ecosystem. Since remote teams are distanced from each other, it is a lot more of a challenge than in real-life situations. Nonetheless, having a company culture is important to how employees and other stakeholders outside the organization perceive you. Having the right culture exhibits core values your company believes in, and this helps form a togetherness and direction for the rest of the team.

PRINCIPLES OF BUILDING THE REMOTE CULTURE

Is the solution complicated? No. But it would take some time to see that result. Establishing a culture is equivalent to nurturing a seed. You need to keep watering it and give it exposure to the sunlight and air before seeing it grow into a big and healthy tree. Building a remote work culture consists of following many principles, and I will share with you the multiple areas you can start working on today. It would also be a good idea to write them down in your planning journal.

Set the Right Foundation

The right remote culture starts with the work environment. When you instill a foundation of trust where everyone has a voice and can share their opinions freely, you are heading in the right direction. Ensure employees have psychological safety by being inclusive of everyone's opinions equally so that there is more togetherness and openness in the group. How can you establish that? Well, that all starts with a leader. It is natural that your group reflects the leader's behavior, and when you start practicing an inclusive and transparent mindset—allowing employees to share thoughts freely and encouraging constructive feedback to improve one another—this forms a strong bond in the team where everyone can trust each other and they are not afraid to speak up when things are going downhill for them. If you continually ask employees for honest feedback, it can help give you valuable insights and you can make adjustments to improve your work process much better than you initially would have.

I'm sure you've had situations where you found it difficult to cope with a situation but felt it wouldn't matter to voice your opinion if the group didn't take it seriously. This is exactly what you can avoid when leading from the front and ensuring no employee feels this way in your group. Additionally, encourage employees to reach out to you anytime and book a one-to-one video meeting at your preferred time slot to discuss any matters that might be bothering them. Proposing this to your group will show that you are a leader who cares for them and is available any time. As a result, you will improve employee engagement and give them a physiological boost that this is a safe circle to work under.

Communicate Company Vision and Work Policies Clearly

Another quality feature that remote organizations should exhibit to employees is transparency. A remote organization with a lack of procedures and clear direction will unsettle employees and make it difficult for them to trust your process. Firstly, communicate the company's mission, vision, and goals clearly and in a concise manner to new employees that join so they buy into the company values early on. I prefer to use the art of storytelling to communicate core values. Keep telling stories regularly, as this is the best way for you to leave a message in your employee's heart for a long time. Storytelling is a powerful skill you can practice if you aren't familiar with it already. Anyone can tell stories, and when you tell inspiring stories that motivate your employees and translate business goals, it gives your team a purpose to keep putting their efforts into daily.

On the other hand, be very clear about your remote work policies. Mention how flexible employees can be or if there is a fixed time daily that employees should dedicate to meeting up with their teams. Making this clear early on will help employees plan their daily work schedule and remove any uncertainty that could hinder their work flow. I have seen remote teams that organize meetings out of nowhere and inform employees very late, thus disrupting their personal space. Make things clear and specific during onboarding so that employees are prepared to utilize their time management skills to deal with the remote work process. Ensure the employees know the right tools to use for common work-related tasks, like using Zoom for team meetings, Slack for internal communication, Asana for project management, etc. When these details are made clear from day one, it will make the right first impression for the employees that this company is the right place to work.

Allow New Employees to Settle

In a remote working scenario, new employees require more time to find their feet and adjust to the company's work processes. Oftentimes, new employees are rushed in and put under constant pressure to figure things out using the right remote tools and to produce results instantly. On top of that, they barely get sufficient training during onboarding and are suddenly expected to work miracles. As a result, this increases employee turnover when they pounce on a chance for another remote-based job. To minimize such situations, it is best to give them a couple of weeks or a maximum of 30 to 60 days to adjust to the working environment. Provide them with smaller projects to work with initially, and then let them work on the more complicated tasks. First up, you can optimize the onboarding training. Make the sessions worth it for the new employees coming through by making clear the remote work policies, the digital tools they will be required to use for specific job functions, and other company processes they will need to know.

In addition, offer them a designated mentor so that they can continually learn on the job and study their peers. Your mentors can be experienced individuals who you have faith in from your team who can take up the job of guiding new employees remotely. Having a mentor for guidance is crucial to help new employees feel at home. Speaking of settling at home, ensure your new employees go through an ice-breaking session to introduce themselves to the team and share their personal interests and hobbies. This makes it easier to settle in and interact with anyone they might bond with remotely. Hence why group onboarding has become a common way of recruiting talent remotely when hiring managers choose to recruit a group of employees together at a time rather than recruiting employees one by one.

Encourage More Interaction

As you are aware, the remote setup contributes to less interaction among employees, and it can often lead to isolation. However, to encourage more interaction, you can set a traditional routine in the form of recurring meetings. Many companies make use of recurring meetings, especially during mornings, called the daily sprint—mostly executed by Agile project teams—to discuss all work-related matters. The recurring nature of these meetings helps employees to look forward to social interaction each day and discuss more about work. One thing to keep in mind is you need to encourage regular two-tiered communication. One is to have regular team interactions within their departments so that they can work constantly to achieve their tasks.

The second thing is to break down barriers within all departments so that it improves coordination, and every employee will know what's going on in the organization, which can be difficult remotely. Recurring meetings can help that. Fix a specific time during the week to carry out these meetings so that employees can manage their calendars and make time for those mandatory team meetings. Remember when I talked about those small coffee breaks where employees make chit-chat? Encourage that more in your remote setup so that employees are encouraged to save contacts of their peers and keep in touch with them. Leverage collaborative tools like Slack to bring more employee interaction and give them room to talk about personal things and hobbies they are passionate about. Ultimately, this gives them the feeling of social freedom and the opportunity to bond with their colleagues.

Give Employee Recognition

I cannot stress enough how important giving your employees recognition helps with the good feel and motivation of your remote camp. Employees crave recognition, and you should have a system in place to recognize their hard work and the success they have brought into the team. For that, you can go with either an employee of the week or month for the best performers, give them an opportunity to deliver a speech, and have them featured on your company's social media to highlight their unique talent. Furthermore, this motivates your current employees to have that burning desire to be the next employee in line to receive recognition. It is great to have healthy competition within your remote team, so provide work-related challenges so that they enhance their performance to stand on top of their competing peers. You can either host individual competitions or divide them into groups and compete. We are social beings, and if you establish some sort of system to encourage competition and provide employee recognition, slowly, employees will buy into it and maximize their productivity, thus bringing more positive results despite everyone working remotely.

Be Creative

When you find creative ways to make your remote employees more involved, it makes your team stand out from the rest of the organization. You don't want your remote workers to only see your company as a place to do work. Feel free to think outside of the box and implement interesting activities to create a close attachment to the company and other remote colleagues. You can try encouraging your remote workers to have cultural-based groups. These can be a book club, gaming club, pet club, anything that many share a passion for. They can have club coordinators and arrange virtual meetings to discuss those topics. Moreover, having regular events where employees get engaged with non-work-related matters makes their experience with the company balanced. If you are a co-located team, you can arrange frequent meetups in real life somewhere enjoyable to improve on that team bonding. If you are a dispersed team—with everyone living in different time zones—this can be tricky, so ensure to have different casual meetings at a time when it suits everyone to meet up and share a few laughs here and there.

WRITING A REMOTE WORK POLICY

A remote work policy is your bread-and-butter document that states all sets of instructions and guidelines for how employees should work remotely. Having this document helps answer all the questions remote employers will have when they join a remote team for the first time—covering everything from all the digital tools they need to have, to when they need to stay online during working hours. Any remote team that wants to be successful will require a remote work policy to inform employees about what is expected of them. It removes any confusion regarding the work process and gives employees clarity to manage their remote work schedule. Ideally, when you prepare a remote work policy, you should consider the following components:

Establish Formal Work Schedules

The first thing to do is to know which positions are suitable for remote work and those which cannot be considered for it. Then, create a work schedule for remote employees which can be either a typical nine-to-five or other flexible timings. This is crucial to let employees know when they should be available. Furthermore, mention a response time expected of employees to respond to their co-workers and clients across communication channels. Making this clear at the start will urge employees to be more proactive and coordinate better remotely.

Set Up a Work Review Process

Assessing one's performance remotely can be tricky, so it is mandatory to mention how an employee's efforts will be measured. Mention clearly the KPIs (key performance indicators) you will use to assess each employee's productivity remotely. Rather than assessing based on the number of working hours, assess their performance based on per task or project completion. This can give them freedom for work flexibility and makes their target achievable in their eyes. Moreover, have an employee review once a week to provide feedback so they can constantly improve. Having a consistent work review process can make it clear for employees that they have a good chance to receive employee recognition remotely and opportunities for promotions.

Clarify Remote Working Conditions

Make sure your remote employees are aware of the rules and the implications when they agree to the remote work policy. This includes letting the employees know how to manage sick days or vacations while working remotely, and the expenses you will cover or not cover when working remotely. When Google first offered a work-from-home policy to its employees, they decided to give $1,000 to each employee so that they could use it to create their ideal remote work setup at home.

Have a Tech Support Guide

The technology is the bedrock of your remote team's productivity and results. Firstly, it is crucial to give them detailed instructions on what tools to use and tutorials on how to use them effectively for their work. Additionally, install antivirus software for cyber security and have everyone sign confidentiality agreements to avoid any data leaks to outside parties. Furthermore, having a tech support team to assist remote employees is absolutely vital. Sort out a tech team to be readily available to remote employees for when they encounter issues with the company software or database.

Conduct Regular Policy Reviews

Finally, keep reviewing your remote work policy regularly and implement changes wherever necessary. Things can change within months, and maybe some positions will be needed or not needed in that time frame. As a result, your remote work policy has to be reviewed thoroughly and reiterated so that new and current employees stay in the loop and don't get confused by any immediate changes.

HOW TO WRITE A REMOTE WORK POLICY

Based on the traits that are expected of a good remote work policy, you can start making an effective work-from-home policy for your remote team. Below is a brief template you can use to write your copy clearly so that remote employees adhere to your conditions.

Template Example

Purpose

State the purpose of this document. It should contain certain terms and conditions for remote employees.

Terms and Conditions:

1. Eligibility

This section talks about whether an employee may be eligible to work remotely based on specific remote working requirements.

2. Company Rules

State that remote employees must adhere to company policies to qualify for working remotely.

3. Expectations

State that employees should follow all the remote work schedules provided and fulfill the minimum working requirements expected regularly.

4. Communication

This section states the availability requirement remote workers should adhere to, including a time frame for responding to coworkers and clients.

5. Insurance and Liability

Mention everything here regarding the health insurance or working compensations covered by the company's remote work policy.

6. Security

State anything to do with data protection, maintaining cybersecurity, providing VPN, and confidentiality agreements.

7. Compensation

Mention here all the compensation that the company will or will not make during an employee's remote work tenure.

Finally, insert a remote employee form at the end of the policy so that employees can fill in their details.

END OF CHAPTER REVIEW

- Building the right culture matters when creating an effective remote ecosystem for employees to thrive in.
- Principles of building a good remote culture include: setting right foundations, communicating work policies clearly, valuing employee onboarding, encouraging more interaction, giving employees recognition, and implementing creative team-building strategies.
- A remote work policy is a detailed document stating all guidelines and working conditions employees must adhere to when working remotely.
- When writing a remote work policy, be sure to include eligibility criteria, a formal work schedule, and a work review process. Clarify all working conditions, offer adequate tech support, and conduct regular policy reviews.

3

REMOTE ONBOARDING—HIRING EMPLOYEES IN THE NEW WORLD ORDER

Once you have laid out the foundations concerning your remote work policy, it is time to learn how to onboard talent that adhere to the remote culture. The year 2020 set the precursor to unprecedented times and gravely affected how things are done, including the hiring process. Read on to find out how modern managers can ensure that they hire and onboard the right talent with optimized use of time and resources in this remote work culture.

HIRING TALENT REMOTELY

When you are used to hiring talent in the physical world, it may seem like a challenge to recruit them remotely. After all, you get fewer insights and lack the human element whenever assessing a candidate this way. Nevertheless, with the tools you have in hand, you can still work your way around it and successfully onboard talented candidates. It is time to leverage the digital era, which can provide you with more information and a wider reach to a formidable global talent pool. Here are a few components you can incorporate into your remote hiring process:

Attend Virtual Career Fairs

Just like attending career fairs in the physical world, you can set up a booth or a virtual lobby in a virtual career fair. Many candidates attend virtual hiring events in search of a job; hence, it is a great opportunity for you to promote your company and discuss the roles you are offering them. Basically, they enter your lobby and it sets up a one-on-one meeting between you and the candidate where you discuss the potential job offers and more about the company's remote work policy. As a result, it is a great opportunity for candidates to understand your work culture and refer your company to their social circle if you request.

Emphasize Face-to-Face Communication

I have seen many recruiters opt to voice call a candidate or turn off their camera when they video interview a bunch of candidates. I get that you want privacy when conducting these activities remotely, but if you want to make a good impression representing your company, I suggest always opting for face-to-face interviews. The big benefit you will get out of having both the cameras on is that you can carefully assess the candidate's body language and reactions to a particular set of questions, thus giving you better insights on the candidate's attitude and confidence level. Moreover, candidates are more appreciative when hiring managers opt to have direct "face time" and keep candidates in the loop. Always try to encourage human interaction regardless of the technology restricting us from doing so.

Prepare Candidates for the Interview

One critical element you can do from your end is to prep the candidates for the interview a day in advance. Candidates are more used to in-person interviews and being successful at them. When it comes to virtual interviews, they may have doubts on how the interview process works. Therefore, prepare the candidates by providing them with video-interview guidelines. This may include telling them about what platform to use (along with a tutorial on how to set up that tool in advance), clarifying whether it's a formal or informal meeting, letting them know what materials they should bring to the interview, advice on adjusting their lighting, and recommending a quiet space for an uninterrupted interview.

Have a Transparent Process

When you are transparent and communicate clearly to the candidate about the hiring process, it saves both your time and theirs. Make it part of your remote hiring process to let the candidate know how many interview rounds there will be in total and when the hiring decision will be made. Moreover, let them know the type of interviews they can expect—like a one-on-one interview or a group interview—in advance. There are a few sites on the internet that host virtual interviews without you needing to be there. It engages the candidates with appropriate questions and even asks for feedback regarding the interview process for making improvements in the future. Lastly, always keep your candidates in the loop. Even if you reject them, be sure to send them an email notifying them of the decision and express gratitude to them for taking their time to participate in the hiring process.

Train Your Hiring Managers

The interviewer is as important as the candidates getting interviewed. When you have a team of hiring managers, coach them so they can stay ahead in their task and successfully conduct numerous interviews. When training your hiring team, make it clear what software they need to install in advance, keep them in the loop by reminding them of the interviews, and provide them with video-interviewing etiquette that can help them get all the insights they need from the candidates. Eventually, you will have an efficient hiring team that can reach out to many candidates and successfully capture those with the right fit.

CONDUCTING A SUCCESSFUL REMOTE INTERVIEW

At times, it can be challenging when you have a poor internet connection or you miss out on asking the most important interview questions. The success of a remote interview can be determined based on whether you have set up the minimum standards to conduct quality interviews and have received adequate insights for making a hiring decision regarding the candidate. Carrying out a successful remote interview is pretty simple once you have incorporated three fundamentals into your remote hiring system.

Leveraging Screen Interaction

One may say it is difficult to gain insights when your candidate is miles away from you, but you can actually leverage interviewing a candidate from behind screens to gain further insights. It may surprise you, but screens give candidates physiological safety, and that helps hiring managers such as yourself to dive deep into the candidate's world and understand them personally.

Usually, hiring managers focus on the IQ and job competencies of the candidates, but you can also use the remote setup as an opportunity to study the Emotional Intelligence of the candidate. Study how they respond to personal distractions around them during the interview and whether they maintain eye contact when asked challenging questions. This will help you to understand if their personality will suit the company's vision and culture. Recruiting from this perspective helps hiring managers find the right candidates who understand how to work remotely and who can contribute value to the organization.

Prepare Your Candidates to Succeed

Candidates will appreciate it if you do your best to help them ease in for the interview and be prepared to successfully represent themselves in front of you. A good way to help them out and make your job easier is sending them pre-interview guidelines. This includes stating which video-conferencing tool to use, how many minutes before the interview they should get logged in, where to sit, how to troubleshoot their system, and what questions they can expect from this interview. As a result of these preparations, the candidates will be able to confidently do their bit and not have any fear of the remote setup that they might feel could potentially tarnish their interview.

Furthermore, when going deep into the talent pool, feel free to broaden your search by inviting candidates that impress you the most, even if they fall short of specific requirements. This might be a candidate you looked up who doesn't have the necessary qualifi-cations or experience for the role, but their cover letter grabbed your attention. If you feel such candidates deserve a chance, feel free to arrange an interview with them to understand their poten-tial. You wouldn't want to overlook some hidden gems in the market by simply looking at the basis of qualifications.

Have a Routine Before Every Interview

Lastly, don't forget about the fact that you're the interviewer and that you should be well-prepared and productive from your end. A fine way to stay consistent with carrying out successful remote interviews is by setting a routine before every interview. Your routine might consist of reviewing the candidate's resume, testing your equipment, microphone, camera quality, and what your zoom background should look like, adjusting your room's lighting, removing any noise or other distractions, and having a list of prepared interview questions. Being prepared for every interview will help you go far in consistently carrying them out successfully. In addition, always look to avoid back-to-back interviews, and try to take at least 10 minutes of break in between consecutive interviews. Use that time to drink, eat, walk around, do some stretching, or go to the bathroom. Having small breaks in between will make sure that you are well-prepared for the next interview without burning yourself out.

TIPS FOR HIRING REMOTELY

Now that you have understood the fundamentals of establishing a successful remote hiring strategy, there are some additional tips you will need to keep in mind to maximize the effectiveness of your onboarding process. Below, you will find a few tips you can consider when preparing your remote hiring process. Use these tips to your advantage wisely.

1. Develop an action plan.

The remote hiring process can be a long process, and it is essential to make sure new employees aren't rushed into the company. Hence why you should adopt an action plan that will include every step, from the number of interview rounds to the orientation process, so that you remove any anxiety from the candidate's end.

2. Start small.

As mentioned in the previous chapter, give employees a period of 30 to 60 days to make themselves feel at home and have ice breaking sessions to build bonds with existing members. This will ensure employees are not put under pressure constantly and have time to get used to the working environment. Conduct small onboarding programs to keep new employees engaged and make them feel more comfortable among their peers.

3. Encourage personal interaction.

Never ignore or leave new employees isolated when they've recently joined the company. This is where you can introduce them to informal settings or events to help them make friends with their peers and share their interests. Allowing new employees to be comfortable and share their story helps them get settled and have existing members excited about their new fellow colleague.

4. Avoid unnecessary layoffs.

Many remote companies find it easy to lay off remote workers and trim down their remote teams. However, consider this twice, as laying off your entire team can cost you a fortune when you have to repeat the process of replacing the lost talent. Before laying off a particular department, assess their performance again and consider your alternatives, whether it is reducing working hours to save costs, or providing better training programs to optimize their performance.

5. Onboard in groups.

When you recruit in groups, it is a great way to minimize redundancies and makes your recruitment process more efficient. Onboarding in cohorts makes it easier to conduct one group interview than doing them one-by-one. And moreover, conducting one training session for the entire cohort instead of providing one-on-one training that can drain resources and time.

6. Give the interview a good makeover.

How your remote space looks to the candidate makes an impression on your company. Therefore, optimize your video background so that it looks more professional and removes any clutter that can be seen from your home office. If your company requires a playful approach, you can use a more vibrant and playful-looking background to make candidates comfortable. Furthermore, always make yourself look smart when interviewing the candidate. Candidates can only see your top half, so ensure you dress professionally and have a good grooming session before meeting up with candidates.

7. Ask for feedback.

When you conduct these interviews initially, you will require some feedback on how to make your process better in the future. Hence, feel free to ask the remote candidate after an interview or after they get onboarded how the recruiting process has gone for them. You can either ask them verbally or send them a questionnaire asking them to rate the experience. This will help you identify what went right or wrong during the hiring process.

8. Be creative with your interviews.

When conducting remote interviews, you do not need to follow the orthodox way of having serious conversations, with awkward silences in between. Find ways to up your interview game by doing some research and keeping up with the latest technology that can help the interviews to be fun and effective. Giving the candidate a memorable interview experience can help you in identifying the right fit and understanding more about their personalities.

9. Streamline your process.

If you could find a way to reduce your recruitment process from four weeks to two weeks, you would take that opportunity and streamline your process. Making your hiring process efficient will help you reduce costs and fulfill your candidate position immediately. Keep reviewing the process and find ways to improve it. Additionally, always keep your process remote so that candidates don't waste time commuting to physical offices and risking their health and safety.

10. Be sure to check the time zone.

Undoubtedly, when you dip your hands into the global talent pool, you will need to consider time zones. Hence why you should make sure you are open to knowing which times candidates are comfortable with and available to have interviews with you and adjust according to their likings. Furthermore, have a Calendly where you can display the times (mentioning the time zone) you are available to conduct an interview so that they can book the right time at their convenience. During the entire hiring process, give priority to time zones and divide candidates into different time zone groups so they get the same experience as everyone else.

FINDING REMOTE EMPLOYEES

Now for the million-dollar question: Where can you find remote employees? Fortunately, thanks to the internet, you don't need to be in a specific region to recruit anyone around the globe. With the internet, you have more options and a wider reach on talent than you would if you were recruiting from one city alone. Apart from the virtual career fair that was discussed earlier in this chapter, here are a few effective ways you can implement to find and reach candidates remotely:

Contact via Their Websites

With the rise of remote jobs, there are many remote workers out there who also offer freelance services during their free time. They create their personal blogs and websites to showcase their portfolio and expertise in the industry. These days, blogs and personal websites act as the modern-day resume for recruiters to have a good insight on the candidate's expertise. You can contact suitable candidates after reviewing their work on their websites by simply checking out their contact page.

Use Social Media

You can reach more potential candidates through social media by exploring specific groups in Facebook, LinkedIn, Twitter, etc. However, make sure you use the right social media platform to reach suitable candidates. If you are looking for design professionals, Pinterest and Dribbble are the best platforms to find top-rated creatives. If you are looking for more experienced professionals, connect with them on LinkedIn or use LinkedIn's talent recruiter to filter and choose the right candidates according to the job role.

Go to Freelancing Platforms

Exploring freelance marketplaces is a fine way to find the most skilled remote workers in a specific niche or industry. Use freelancing platforms such as Fiverr, Upwork, and Freelancer to find top-skilled professionals so you can set up a one-on-one discussion with them. It may be tricky to convince a freelancer for a full-time position if they choose to freelance full-time; hence, you can contract them as freelancers for your firm and maintain long-term working relationships since they are affordable and chargeable on a per-project basis.

Job Boards

Job sites are a great way of getting leads when you open a job post on the website. Make sure to create a clear job description explaining all the qualification requirements, company policy, hiring procedure, compensation, and contact information. Having all this information present raises the chances of candidates applying to your job post and seeing you as a reputable remote organization.

Here is a list of a few remote-based job boards you can start exploring now:

- Flexjobs
- Remote.co
- Indeed
- Glassdoor
- Arc
- We Work Remotely
- Career Vault
- Authentic Jobs
- Jobspresso

- Remote OK
- JustRemote

Use your Network

After going through all these platforms, maybe your suitable candidate is present in your network itself. Go through your personal and professional network first to seek out suitable remote workers that will fulfill the job role. You can go through your current LinkedIn connections or speak to your friends. Moreover, you can recruit internally by promoting current remote employees or asking your colleagues to refer to the job via their personal network.

END OF CHAPTER REVIEW

- Use virtual career fairs to set up an online booth and have one-on-one conversations with the candidate about your company culture and remote positions.
- Ensure you have a transparent and interactive remote recruitment process. Always look to set up your candidates for success by providing pre-interview guidelines and tips.
- Set a routine before conducting interviews. Review the candidate's resume, test your equipment, remove distractions, adjust your space, and have interview questions prepared. Moreover, make sure to take small breaks in between consecutive interviews.
- Develop an action plan, start small, encourage personal interaction, and streamline your hiring process to make it more efficient. You can consider onboarding in groups

to save resources, and consider the candidates' time zones during the entire process.

- There are lots of ways in which you can find suitable remote workers online. You can reach them through their blogs, websites, social media, freelancing platforms, job boards, and you can also find some through your personal and professional network.

4

WELCOMING THE TALENT
ONBOARD

After the remote hiring process, it is time to welcome the new talent onboard. This chapter is dedicated to remote onboarding. Read on to learn important tips and suggestions to ensure that the hired talent feels welcomed in the organization and is aligned with the organization's goals and mission right from the start.

REMOTE ONBOARDING: AN OVERVIEW

Just like in person, you'll have your employee onboarding process where new employees take the time to learn the job role and team members and absorb the company's culture and goals. It may seem like an easier process when new employees are constantly present in the office daily and learning their tasks quickly. Remote onboarding is a different challenge where the process needs to be precise and ensure remote employees are settled in with ease. It is extremely crucial to have a proper onboarding strategy, as it can help to maximize new employees' productivity, encourage them to bond with team members quickly, and remove any anxiety they may have about the organization. It was found that companies that had better onboarding strategies retained their employees longer compared to companies with poor or no onboarding strategies at all.

Formal remote onboarding consists of formal meetings, guidelines, and a set of instructional training that new employees benefit from. Whereas informal remote onboarding sessions are mainly to do with casual team-building meetings and ice-breaking sessions for new employees to be more comfortable and feel like part of the family. Companies usually look to incorporate a mixed strategy of having both formal and informal settings to create a satisfying experience for the onboarders while making sure they get the point across of what is expected of them in the job. Onboarding shouldn't be confused with orientation—which is a one-time event—whereas onboarding is a series of events and activities conducted in a specific duration.

Giving Time to Settle

Typically, a remote onboarding session can go from a minimum of two weeks and up to 60 days. In some cases, it can take up to several months for employees to get used to their surroundings and become part of the team. It is essential to give new employees the time they deserve to slowly integrate into the team and learn from their experienced peers from the start. The onboarding duration can depend on the job role or specific department they belong to.

Depending on the nature of the task, some employees may require less than a month to adjust, while others may need many months to adjust to the organizational climate. Nevertheless, if you elongate the onboarding process for up to a year, it maximizes employee retention better because they will have enough time to become part of the team's core. Ensure that new employees are inducted into their teams without adding any pressure early on and provide enough support for them to grow and improve as a collective.

Challenges of Remote Onboarding

It is not an easy process to implement when there are challenges that await when onboarding new hires. Firstly, keep them briefed with the technical requirements expected in their job. By providing tutorials and continuous technical support, it can help new hires to feel less anxious about the technical side of things. In addition, keeping them always socially engaged with the team can be a huge task. It is easy for new hires to be left out and completely isolated from their teams due to the remote nature. However, having a series of recurring meetings and assigning them a buddy or a mentor can help new hires to adjust to the team mechanics and feel like part of the family.

In a nutshell, it is never easy, and you shouldn't expect new employees to quickly get the company culture and organizational goals, especially when there is no physical environment, and it can take some time to learn remotely. Many remote organizations run out of patience and tend to give up on new hires when they do not produce results instantly because they never gave them adequate time and resources to onboard properly.

TIPS FOR SUCCESSFUL ONBOARDING

Most managers such as yourself will be aware by now that remote onboarding can be an uphill challenge and something that you need to get right to retain those employees for the long-term. Fortunately for you, we have a few tips you can implement during your remote team onboarding process so new hires can start on the right foot.

Start off Quickly

You can be pretty sure that the night before their first day, new hires will have a lot of anxiety and won't know what to fully expect on day one. That anxiety could grow if they're not fully informed about their role, the company culture, or introduced to the team. Therefore, the best way to start off positively is to ensure new hires quickly are exposed to as much information about the company and team as possible from day one. This includes showing that first impression during the hiring process as well. Have the new employee added to Slack immediately, encouraged to have their work-related software set up, a mentor or buddy assigned, and an introductory video to welcome them. Additionally, provide them with a small project to work with in the first week so they feel excited to show their potential to the team. It is crucial to create a positive connection with the company from day one so new hires can ease into the process and feel exhilarated to be part of the company culture.

Build Relationships

In the physical world, relationships can be formed quite organically when new hires spend time with others in the office. On the other hand, you will need a proactive measure to involve new hires with current employees as early as possible in the remote setting. In the remote setup, it is easy for the new hire to be left out while the current employees are engaged with their routine tasks. Therefore, look to involve the new hires in groups as early as possible (without any added pressure), so they can understand the team dynamics and slowly bond with other team members. Moreover, it is crucial they build one-on-one relationships as well with their co-workers. Remote teams should make good use of both formal and informal settings to keep the new hires online during the early stages of onboarding and keep them engaged with others.

Trust is formed on day one, when the new hires are able to easily build good relationships with their co-workers. To make the process even smoother, try to designate an experienced member from your team to keep an eye on the new hires and guide them through these early stages as an online buddy. As a result, this helps new hires to be open up with their buddy and learn more about the work processes. However, building relationships shouldn't limit them to their co-workers alone. Have them involved more with their supervisors or bosses so they form good, formal relationships there. In addition, introduce them to various other stakeholders of the company when the new employees get involved early on in smaller projects.

Promote the Company Culture

During these early onboarding stages, the new hires will be at their peak interest and enthusiasm levels. They will be curious to learn more about their work and justify their position in the company. Therefore, you must make sure they go along with that flow by imprinting the company culture on their minds early on. As for the previous point, try to assign one experienced member from your team to guide the new hires and explain more about the company culture and how everything works. Be sure to develop a feedback mechanism so that they can feel free to ask questions and learn more about the culture.

When you onboard new hires, you can arrange a separate session for everyone to ask questions about the company's history, core values, objectives, goals, and various other work processes. It can help the new group get involved and excited about learning more about their new company. Another strategy could be documenting a company culture handbook that illustrates everything the new hires need to know about the company. This content can be a mix of text documents, videos, and even a gamified learning experience. In a nutshell, don't leave your new employees trying to solve the company as a mysterious puzzle. Make sure everything is transparent to them from day one.

Set Clear Expectations

The onboarding process is critical in determining whether the new hire will become a success over the long run for the organization. To achieve a positive outcome, they need to get off to a great start to build that momentum, and a good way to do that is by setting up a realistic target in their minds. In the first week, there should be clear expectations communicated to the new hires illustrating what success should look like in the next 30 to 60 days for them. In addition, you should communicate the potential growth they can achieve during their time with the company, which includes promotions, pay raises, performance bonuses, etc.

Setting these expectations clearly motivates the employees to start on their best foot immediately and make career growth plans for themselves. If you hadn't communicated any expectations to them, they would not exhibit that drive to build momentum in their work and would have their positions in the company left in uncertainty. When communicating these expectations, ensure they are achievable, realistic, and smaller milestones so they don't feel over-pressured from the beginning.

Encourage Learning and Development

During the onboarding program, it is extremely important to provide employees with sufficient training. Remote workers, similar to traditional workers, look for personal and career growth in whichever company they work with. You can provide this in two ways. The first way is to provide them with several training sessions with a designated mentor or industry expert. Have several one-on-one and group activities to train each individual so they get used to their job role. The other way is to have learning and development software that provides training materials and other resources for them so they can study at their own pace. Nonetheless, having these training programs can help them settle in and understand their job role well.

To add to that point, I am sure that you want the employees to succeed with the company and to retain them for many years rather than leaving them isolated and working miracles on the job. In addition, it is useful to have frequent training sessions and programs later on in their onboarding sessions and after a year or so in the company. This helps them to keep up with the industry requirements in this ever-changing market and upgrade their skills for further career growth. Your employees will stay longer with you —regardless of a remote setup—if you provide frequent training sessions, as well as learning and development programs for their personal and professional growth.

Sense of Belonging

Employees want to feel that they rightfully belong where they are. It is natural to see new hires having a little bit of imposter syndrome and being left isolated when they have no one to share their feelings with. This can happen quite easily remotely, and hence, you should encourage new hires and help them believe that they belong to the company at the very start. A great way to do this is to add them to all communication channels as soon as possible and get them involved with their co-workers both formally and informally. Have a separate meeting or communication channel for them to build casual bonds and share their personal hobbies and interests with existing employees so they feel part of the family.

One fine idea you can try is hosting virtual lunches so that new employees can casually bond with existing members, as we organically bond whenever we feast together. Or else assign them a mentor or buddy to provide someone they can feel free to talk to anytime. Make sure the new employees feel at home to encourage them to stay with the company for a long time rather than being alienated. This can easily happen in a remote setup, so it is essential to give equal attention to all new hires during the initial onboarding stages so that they don't feel isolated and regret their decision to join the company.

Stimulate Collaborative Learning

To encourage more teamwork and maintain consistent team dynamics, new hires should be integrated into the team early on so they can learn their role and how each department communicates with each other. You should involve new hires in group projects during onboarding stages so that they can build relationships with their team members from day one. Additionally, help them understand how each department works with one another and which contacts they need to save so they can be more efficient with their communication. Make use of good online collaborative tools so that employees will have an easy time adjusting and freely coordinating with other team members.

MAKE THEM FEEL AT HOME

Naturally, welcoming someone remotely won't have that same vibe to it compared to welcoming someone on a first day in the office. You will need to replicate office-based scenarios that they experience in real life virtually so that they can feel the same energy and be excited for the job. A warm welcome combined with happy smiles all around is a good way to make a positive first impression, and they will reflect back positive vibes. From day one, send them all the resources they need virtually or to their homes with a warm welcome message. Have existing employees prepare introductory videos for new hires to make them feel more at home. Or invite them to that virtual lunch I mentioned on the first day itself. The first day or week during their onboarding is critical, and you will need to put a lot of effort into making them feel like they're already part of the family.

Introduce them to Existing Members

Assist them in meeting their co-workers and building bonds instantly. When they get invited to their first team meeting, ensure before any formal discussions that the new members are given a chance to introduce themselves and have informal chats with their co-workers. In sports teams, new members to the team are made to sing a song during their induction, so the same can be implemented in your team in the form of cultural activities. Have new employees sing a song, play an instrument, tell a story, or share any other passionate hobbies they have so they feel part of the group and other existing members will know more about them.

Communicate the Plan Across the Organization

Ensure you solidify your onboarding plan and don't keep every plan to yourself or share only with the HR team. The plan should be communicated across all departments so teams will be aware of the new employees joining their teams and can implement onboarding strategies wherever necessary. There can be instances where your marketing manager forgets to introduce the new hire because he wasn't aware of a new team member or wasn't instructed to follow that guideline. This all stems from having a strong company culture and structure for everyone to be onboard with your plans. Hence, pass on the message to every department manager about new recruits and keep them updated. Coach them on how to welcome new members on their first day and how to support them during the initial months. Dedicate a team meeting with department managers to working on this aspect so that everyone will know how to treat their new hires and support them throughout their onboarding period.

Keep Checking in

In real life, you can have regular coffee breaks or stop by at someone's desk to check how they're doing. In the virtual world, however, this can be difficult because we respect one's privacy but at the same time we need to check on the new hires to see if they need any help. Thus, develop a system where the new hires can check in with their managers or mentors daily about what they did and ask questions they have regarding their work. These sessions will help them clarify all the doubts and anxieties they may have had during their first few days and get things off their chest. Another great alternative is to assign them an online buddy. A buddy is someone they can be more personal with and communicate with more freely anytime. There are two types of buddies you can adopt with the new hires—role buddy or culture buddy. A role buddy is one who works closely with the onboarding program and mentors new hires to adjust to the work process and the overall work-life balance. Whereas the culture buddy is someone who will educate the new hires on the company's values, history, and goals they aim to achieve.

Finishing Touches

Lastly, review all the necessary legal documentation and guidelines regarding the new hires. When managing remotely, you will need to keep a good eye on these things and keep up to date with the laws of your governing area. New hires shouldn't be involved in any legal difficulties, so it is up to you or the legal team to sort all those out, such as their employment identification and other legal paperwork. Leverage technology to get digital paperwork signed easily with digital signatures. Encourage employees to go green and use the digital tools they are supposed to work with. Review all the technical requirements for them by sending them clearly explained tutorials and giving them the helpline number to contact tech support. Once you have set up everything for the new hires, they can confidently start learning and performing beyond their expectations because you gave them a great head start to succeed thanks to your onboarding program.

END OF CHAPTER REVIEW

- An employee onboarding is where new hires take the time to learn the job role and team members and absorb the company's culture and goals.
- Formal onboarding consists of formal meetings, guidelines, and a set of instructional training. Whereas informal onboarding has mainly to do with casual team-building meetings and ice-breaking sessions for new employees to be part of the family.
- It is essential to have new hires start their journey quickly by forming relationships across the organization and getting a sense of belonging.
- Set clear expectations for the new hires and explain the company culture so they know what is expected of them.

- Assign new hires a buddy or a mentor so they have someone to talk to and learn from about their job role or company values.
- Communicate the onboarding plan across all departments so every manager knows what to do to make new hires feel welcomed in their new teams.

5

ENCOURAGING COMMUNICATION

Communication is the key to success for organizations across different verticals. The new remote work culture has posed several challenges to effective communication. Both the work force and their managers are having a hard time communicating effectively and ensuring a smooth flow of work. This chapter will highlight the significance of uninterrupted communication in the remote work culture and offers strategies to build clear communication lines throughout the organization.

REMOTE COMMUNICATION

Remote communication is another way of communicating digitally when your employees are miles apart from each other. You will make use of digital tools to communicate with fellow remote workers and work together as a team to achieve organizational goals. In a nutshell, you must aim to have a digital workspace that acts as a unified collaboration network for remote workers to coordinate with one another.

It is crucial to have clear communication—especially with the remote work environment—because it can bring positive results to your remote team and maximize team efficiency. Establishing effective and clear remote communication is building the foundation of an effective virtual team.

Challenges of Communicating Remotely

Without a doubt, it can be tricky to communicate with co-workers when we are all at our own homes and miles apart from each other. The non-verbal communication—that which consists of body language and visual cues—make up more than 50% of our typical face-to-face communication. As you can see, this is one of the biggest challenges to tackle already with the remote work culture, which inhibits our non-verbal communication most of the time. With little to no contact with our colleagues and bosses, a remote worker can easily feel disconnected and isolated when compared to working in a traditional office, where colleagues drop by each other's desks or cubicles from time to time.

With dispersed teams, they will need to tackle the issue of coordination when team members belong to different time zones. If a member from the American region communicates with those from Asia, it might take a while to get a response due to living in different time zones. As a result, this can have an effect and delay performance in many remote teams. On top of that, technical issues such as poor connectivity or outdated communication tools can result in unnecessary misunderstandings and disputes among teams. This is something you don't want, especially when it has to do with the technology aspect of things.

Managers Can Take the Lead

Sometimes, over-communication can be a problem when a remote employee has several complaints and queries for the staff. This can lead to more disruptions in the work-life balance when there is no effective remote communication strategy put into place. Hence, managers should adopt measures to improve remote communication and avoid any disputes that occur as a result of it. Devising clear communication plans is a start managers such as yourself should look into implementing early on. This can be solved by bringing employees into one unified platform to communicate rather than having them use multiple communication tools that are all over the place. Employees can get overwhelmed in that situation. Therefore, have them use mandatory communication tools for specific situations. If you can bring them over to one platform where they can communicate about any work or non-work-related aspects, the better. Integration of the communication channels is a must to improve efficiency among your remote team members.

To avoid miscommunication and misunderstanding, messages should be sent in a clear and concise manner. Many feel that sending emojis makes you look unprofessional, but in my opinion, you should encourage the use of emojis so it contextualizes the message. Many times, we find it difficult to understand the tone and meaning of text messages because, unlike face-to-face communication, we can't see any non-verbal cues. Using emojis along with concise messages can help team members avoid misinterpretation.

Ensure that employees have a virtual space designated for work-related aspects and another one for casual talk. Slack is a good tool to sort out work channels, including one designated water cooler channel for employees to share GIFs, memes, and viral videos, thus enjoying themselves.

GETTING EMPLOYEES MORE CONNECTED

When you engage a remote workforce, it results in extraordinary performances in the long run. This is only possible when you have a clear remote communication strategy to make remote workers feel more connected with the current work culture. Here are a few tips you can start jotting down in your plans to make remote employees more communicative and integrated with the business:

Open line of communication

Communication is a two-way process, so it is mandatory to keep an open line of communication with your team. Ensure that your voice can be heard by them and also that their voice can be heard by you. Instill a feedback mechanism into the communication process to gain further insights. Providing honest and constructive feedback shows that you are paying attention to your team's efforts and that they are providing you with insights on where things can be improved. Having this system makes everything better for the team.

Utilize collaborative tools

Unsurprisingly, you will need to be equipped with reliable collaborative tools to make sure your remote workforce communicates effectively and efficiently to achieve their tasks. For that, you need to make clear which remote communication tools everyone should use collectively. For messaging, your team could use Slack, which integrates both collaborative and private communication. For work collaboration, your team can use software like ERP or project management tools like Asana, Notion, etc., while having a good cloud-based storage tool as backup to safely store data like

Google drive or OneDrive. Use these communication tools to support and boost team engagement.

Hold recurring meetings

Habits form lifestyle. Lifestyle breeds results. By holding regular face-to-face meetings remotely, you are making a habit of employees seeing each other regularly. In addition, it helps you, as a manager, to understand your team better and keep up to date with the current and future projects. Hence why organizing a daily morning sprint would be beneficial for you and your team. If your team wants more space and flexibility, try to host two or three meetings per week so that everyone is kept up to date with what's going on in the company. Make use of video-conferencing tools like Zoom, Skype, and Microsoft Teams to host recurring meetings with your team.

Be transparent when communicating

Transparency is key for effective communication. Hence why you should encourage members to respond to co-workers' messages and not leave team members hanging. Make use of emojis and clear texts to convey your message so that everyone understands what's expected. When writing texts, make use of smaller paragraphs or fewer sentences so remote employees can easily scan your text. They can be put off when they see large blocks of texts. When doing face-to-face meetings, check in with them regularly and ask every member if they fully understand what has been said. Invite questions anytime so that everyone is made clear on what is being discussed.

Provide employees with flexibility

When you give your employees the freedom to manage their work schedules, this can create a better understanding with the team. For example, have your employees set a time on Slack when they will always be available and online. Employees could be busy with their work, taking care of children, cooking, etc., thus tackling their personal lives along with work. Therefore, allow employees to communicate their peak availability so that the quality of communication improves among the team. In addition, you can assign your employees a mentor whom they can keep in touch with based on their availability so that they will be aware of important things. A mentorship program is essential when onboarding new hires.

Incorporate the fun and playful factor

When you add some fun traditions for your team, you are boosting team engagement and work/life balance. A fun tradition you can implement is wishing employees a happy birthday. If you are a co-located team, you can have a cake party at the office. In addition to that, have a designated channel where employees can have fun and have casual conversations. You must give employees some degree of freedom to let them talk about non-work-related matters in their spare time to improve team-bonding.

Bring the team together

Always take time to recognize each team member's efforts and accomplishments. This can be a simple "well done" or a round of applause at the end of a meeting for a particular team member who did their work brilliantly. Giving recognition can boost other employees' productivity and motivation to another level. They will have more hunger to achieve success and crave that positive recognition. Hence, implement an employee of the week or month scheme to reward employees frequently. Furthermore, to improve team bonding and cohesiveness, plan a yearly or monthly real-life meeting. This is applicable mostly for co-located teams due to logistics. Have your team members get together for lunch, dinner, or have fun at parks. As a result, this opportunity will help members to learn more about each other and be more unified as a team.

MANAGERS CAN BOOST EFFECTIVE COMMUNICATION

As a manager, you can maximize effective communication by utilizing these methods and soft skills:

Adopt the right technology for communicating.

First and foremost, ensure your team is equipped with the right technology and communication tools to collaborate efficiently. This point will be covered in depth in the next section, so I will keep this brief for now.

Establish goals and expectations.

When you make your goals and expectations clear to your remote team, this means you are communicating clearly regarding the project. When the team is aware of the specifics, this gives them direction and they will know the target that needs to be achieved.

Communicate the message clearly.

Ensure you deliver your message as clearly as possible to your remote team. Adopt the right communication channels to make sure remote employees can receive and convey messages. If it is a formal memo, use an email. If it is personal advice, use private messaging. Make the language and sentences concise for clear interpretation.

Keep everyone actively engaged.

Another fine trait of a manager is their ability to keep their group involved and boost engagement. For that, you need to make sure all communication lines are kept open and accessible to everyone. Create a work culture where you encourage continuous back-and-forth dialogue and maintain discussions among team members. As a result, that will spur other members of your team to join in on the conversation and be involved more.

Keep listening to your team.

Always keep both your ears open for your team members or other colleagues. You must be ready to welcome any opinions, even if you do not agree with them. Moreover, taking in suggestions and important feedback can help you find solutions to solve specific issues, and it also conveys a message to your team that you are an open-minded leader.

Don't micromanage your employees.

Micromanaging remotely can seem as difficult and more of an annoyance for the employee compared to when you walk up to someone many times at their desk. It is pretty obvious when an employee is bombarded with countless calls, messages, and emails from their boss. As a result, it makes their experience uncomfortable. As a manager, respect your employees' space and trust them to do their job. You can check in a few times on them daily depending on the urgency of the task, but never cross the limit.

Utilize team-building activities.

One fine way to boost employee engagement and team cohesiveness is by implementing virtual team-building activities into your daily work routine. This can be possible by dividing your employees into groups for an upcoming project and telling them to work as a team and meet up often. Furthermore, you can add a competitive spice to these team-building activities by rewarding the best performing team with an appreciation post or a small office party (for co-located teams).

Give them time to cool off.

You know where this is going, and yes, you should establish a water cooler for your employees virtually. Create a separate channel or dedicated video meeting for employees to hang out and discuss casual things. Giving them a break from work restores some balance to their schedule and helps them work on their communication with their team.

Use one-on-one messaging to your advantage.

Some employees may not speak up during meetings and are more comfortable with one-on-one messaging. When you understand which employees require that, take advantage of that communication channel so you can get the best out of them and keep communication lines open with them. In addition, you should look to leverage this technique with every team member you want to speak with privately, as this gives them a safe space to open up with you and share important work and personal details you may need to know.

Have a reliable support system set up.

Just like customer care helplines, have a continuous support system for your employees for any work-related issues and further queries. In a remote setup, there will be frequent technical and other issues encountered by your employees, so it is essential to give them support through a helpline or communication bot to assist them with anything they need help with.

REMOTE TOOLS FOR INSTANT COMMUNICATION

With numerous online and remote tools available, it can be a tricky situation to decide which tool will work best for you. In fact, there are loads out there that can help you successfully communicate with your remote team. Having the right tools available to you can help boost spontaneous communication and team morale. Hence why communication is an integral part of a business's success.

Methods of Remote Communication

Remote teams use various strategies and communication tools to collaborate. However, I've narrowed down the most essential methods of remote communication you will need to tick off in your checklist to ensure your team is well supported in every aspect.

Instant Messaging

Firstly, encourage employees to use instant messaging to communicate with co-workers instantly. It's an efficient remote communication method one can use for informal discussions and building relationships.

Email

As for formal communication, emails are definitely a must-have method of communication for your team. Despite the fact that it is not a spontaneous way of communicating, it gives you more room to draft a big message and put some thought into it when replying.

Meetings

Make use of video-conferencing tools to have face-to-face discussions, which can help a great deal in understanding non-verbal cues and the body language of a person. Your typical meetings can be either video or audio calls depending on the situation. It is crucial to keep scheduling and hosting recurring meetings for smooth communication flow.

Collaborative software

Using collaborative software can help your team stay more organized, as it helps in sending messages as well as sharing work documents and project details efficiently. In addition, collaborative software offers multiple channels for work and non-work-related activities; hence, it would be great to set up a virtual water cooler for employees to take a break from work when they need to and to chat with other co-workers.

Project management tools

Similar to collaborative software, project management software helps in organizing business projects in terms of planning, scheduling, milestones, file-sharing, progress, reports, etc. Additionally, it includes a communication channel for team members to collaborate and make them more efficient in completing multiple projects.

Daily reports

Another fine method of communication and keeping track of what your employees have completed is asking them to submit digital reports daily. In fact, there is tracking software that allows you to measure a remote employee's daily activities and monitor your team's overall progress. Make use of activity-based reports and provide a template for your team to fill in regularly.

Presentations

Other than video conferences, making use of presentations and visual diagrams is a good way of communicating your messages to the team and organization. It makes sharing ideas innovative and allows members to store the presentations in their own files so they can refer to them whenever they need to. In addition, recording meetings and other video conferences helps team members who might have missed the meetings to refer back to them if they are unclear about anything.

Communication Tools for Remote Teams

Here are some of the best remote communication tools that are commonly used by remote teams today. These will help you maximize your team's communication effectively:

- Zoom
- Slack
- Microsoft Teams
- Google Hangouts
- GoToMeeting
- Basecamp3
- FreeConference
- Dialpad
- Gather
- JoinMe

END OF CHAPTER REVIEW

- It is crucial to have clear communication—especially with the remote work environment—because it can bring positive results to your remote team and maximize team efficiency.
- Some of the communication challenges of remote-based teams include lack of non-verbal communication, members being from different time zones, misinterpretation, miscommunication leading to disputes, and sometimes over communicating.
- Keep an open line of communication, encourage feedback, and utilize collaborative tools to clearly convey messages and coordinate better as a team.
- Adopt the right tools and methods for remote communication. Allow your employees to be flexible and give them time for non-work-related communication.
- Make use of instant messaging, emails, recurring meetings, collaborative software, project management tools, presentations, and activity reports for an all-round effective communication.

- Some of the best remote tools for communication include Zoom, Slack, Microsoft Teams, Google Hangouts, GoToMeeting, Basecamp3, Dialpad, FreeConference, JoinMe, and Gather.

6

MANAGING REMOTE MEETINGS

W e will continue diving deep into the communication aspect of things and how it has been a key challenge that most remote managers face. This chapter provides a comprehensive walkthrough of conducting effective communication through remote meetings and offers tools to achieve this.

ADVANTAGES OF REMOTE MEETINGS

Virtual meetings are easy to set up, and it is a fine way to communicate between remote employees. It makes use of technology to collaborate in real-time with one another so the team can collectively accomplish an objective. The best part is that all you need is a microphone and a camera installed in your device, and you are good to go. Having remote virtual meetings regularly is crucial for the overall coordination and communication of the business. Let us look through some of the advantages of using remote meetings regularly as a communication channel.

Improves Communication

No-brainer here! Remote meetings are one of the best ways to improve your communication, as it encourages both internal and external communication. You can reach co-workers internally and clients or other stakeholders externally. When you meet people face-to-face on the screen, you are more likely to pick up non-verbal cues and have more effective communication. When you have a moderator (who can be you or someone you assign) controlling the meeting and not letting everyone's voices disrupt the flow of the conversation, you have a powerful remote communication line in your arsenal.

Minimizes Costs

Since video meetings are done remotely, this means you are not commuting to the office daily and spending all that money on travel and office expenses. As a result, virtual meetings cut down on those expenses and save you a lot more money than you might think. The biggest benefit of video-conferencing tools is that most of them are free of charge to get started, and their premium packages are way cheaper compared to the monthly expenses you would need to spend on transportation and operational costs when attending these meetings. Moreover, it benefits the pockets of other co-workers as well when they can attend their meetings from home.

Enhances Efficiency

Remote meetings are a perfect hack to improve productivity and help a remote team be more efficient in their work. When you conduct regular meetings, there's many processes that go into them, such as getting the staff together, waiting for some stragglers, having some snacks prepared, walking to the meeting room, etc. With a remote setup, everyone has the tools to be more efficient and boost their meeting productivity. There will be chat boxes for anyone who didn't have a chance to speak up in meetings to get a point across. As a result, this improves the meeting's effectiveness and enhances everyone's performance.

Saves Time

Take the example of a sales representative having scheduled five meetings with their clients. If this was a traditional setting, the sales representative would have to commute for hours, going from office to office to meet these clients. By the time it is sunset, they might have only been able to complete three meetings due to reasons such as traffic, going to a restaurant to have lunch, waiting in the client's lobby, distance from client A to client B, etc. However, if they had conducted all these meetings virtually, there is a great chance that the sales representative would have finished all five of them within a couple of hours, thus giving them time and energy to conduct more meetings and reach more customers. As you can see from this example, undoubtedly, conducting more remote meetings will significantly save more time for the business.

Encourages Organizational Collaboration

This is something you will love about remote meetings, which is their ability to unify an organization and have transparent communication. Thanks to these digital tools, you will not need to rely on anyone from your organization to set up a meeting with a manager from another department. Anyone will be reachable and more willing to take a few minutes for a virtual meeting, and, as a result, this improves the team and organizational collaboration massively. Furthermore, it allows teams across various departments to chat, share important files, and validate reports a lot quicker than they would in a physical environment.

Well-Structured Medium

Another benefit of having virtual meetings is they will eliminate the fluff and get straight to the point. It adds more structure and focus, since each meeting will have a clear agenda and everyone knows what to discuss and expect from these meetings. Moreover, you can keep adding these structured meetings multiple times within a space of a few minutes and expect to get your points across to everyone. One more point to mention, since virtual meetings add structure, it is quite rare to have unsuccessful remote meetings compared to the traditional face-to-face way. You won't find anyone leaving or rescheduling the meeting for later on, since most of the time everyone will have understood every detail discussed in the meeting and can refer to recordings if they forget any details (of course, recording a meeting should be agreed on with the opposite party if having a one-on-one meeting).

Wider Reach

Lastly, as you have guessed, you can reach and meet many people around the globe anytime. Hence why virtual meetings are a great way to build foreign business connections, find talent that wouldn't be available in the host country, and globally reach customers from a marketing standpoint. Having virtual meetings means barriers are cut down and there are endless possibilities to ensure your business gets to the potential heights it can achieve.

IMPORTANT TYPES OF REMOTE MEETINGS

Now that you have discovered the difference between remote meetings and face-to-face meetings and how it significantly improves productivity and efficiency, here are a few remote meeting types that are essential for your team's success and frequent collaboration. A couple of them are usually adopted by agile project management teams in tech companies. However, for any business, you can adopt any of these methods and tweak them according to the industry you belong to.

One-on-One Meeting

Let's start with the simplest one and probably the most effective method that you can use (remember leveraging one-on-one messaging in the previous chapter). Having one-on-one virtual meetings allows managers such as yourself to understand and build relationships with your co-workers better. Moreover, it gives a safe space for your team members or clients to share their thoughts and feelings, thus giving you effective meetings most of the time you opt for this method. There is no limitation on having one-on-ones, and you can schedule them many times in a day. When your business offers a mentorship program to your new hires or clients, one-on-ones are the most efficient and effective way to build rapport and provide value to someone.

Daily Stand-Ups

When it comes to daily meetings like the stand-ups, this gives remote teams an opportunity to reflect and discuss regularly regarding many business obstacles and to find solutions to those problems. It may seem like the daily morning meetings can frustrate some of your team, but it is a habit that your remote team should get used to. In the long run, it improves team collaboration, since everyone will be used to attending these meetings and communicating regularly. Furthermore, it is a good way to speed up project deadlines and create urgency within a team when a point is raised every single day in the stand-ups.

Weekly Meetings

Your weekly meetings can depend on the projects you and your team are working on. If they don't require you to meet up daily but do require frequent communication, then weekly meetings meet these expectations. It is usually best to have weekly meetings fixed on a specific day so that everyone will be aware and manage their schedule to attend those meetings. But in some cases, project teams tend to pack weekly meetings closer to a project deadline or conduct them out of the blue during emergency situations.

Retrospectives

Something that you can pick up from agile teams is incorporating retrospective meetings into your remote team. Simply put, a retrospective is a brief meeting where a project team comes together to reflect on their last sprint and discuss ways to improve their next one. This is a progressive ideology that many businesses, despite the industry they belong to, should adopt in their routines. Basically, you and your team should discuss what went good, what went bad, brainstorm new ideas, and finally develop action plans for the upcoming sprint. These meetings can be adapted into your remote team schedule once every two weeks and are not necessary to have daily; unless, of course, the nature of your project calls upon having frequent meetings in a tight schedule.

Design Sprints

This will catch the eye of many product managers and design teams out there. Frankly speaking, a design sprint is a concentrated meeting among design teams to design and validate prototypes within only five days. If your business is not into designing, this idea can be adapted into the industry you belong to. This is useful for project teams that want to be more efficient and produce results quickly. With the help of frequent remote meetings, your regular design sprints can be successful, as you will have your remote team meet up daily sharing their ideas, developing strategies, designing solutions, and finally validating the results.

VIRTUAL MEETING ETIQUETTE FOR EFFECTIVE COMMUNICATION

To provide effective meetings, one must know how to conduct them professionally. Oftentimes, there can be technical disruptions, or maybe the host arrives late, thus upsetting a lot of people. To avoid such mistakes, you will be provided with 11 remote meeting tips that you can incorporate into your regular meetings to make the sessions more effective, giving everyone a pleasant experience.

1. Define the need.

First and foremost, you must be aware of whether you actually need a remote meeting in the first place. Sometimes, it becomes a waste of someone's valuable time when you schedule a meeting only to find out that it wasn't worth the hassle. Therefore, you must have a solid reason that convinces attendees that a meeting will be worth attending and that they will get value from it. Here are a few ways you can go about defining your needs. Firstly, find out if you can solve your potential problem without the need for gathering everyone for a virtual meeting. If the answer is yes, then there is no point in having one and you can solve the issue all by yourself. If not, then ask yourself whether you need to raise this issue urgently or let it wait. Depending on the answer to that, you can then ask yourself if this can be done through a much simpler strategy than having everyone gathered for a meeting. If this is something you can solve instantly through email or instant messaging, then you should adopt that route instead. However, if those won't satisfy the problem and you require a virtual meeting, then you probably have a good reason to convince your attendees to attend this meeting.

2. Narrow down attendees.

Once you have defined your need carefully, assess who all needs to attend this meeting. If this is a crucial meeting that requires only your sales and marketing staff to attend, then there is no need for your finance team to waste their time and attend a meeting that they will get no value from. Hence, be selective and invite attendees who you believe will get value out of this meeting. It can be unpleasant if you invite someone for the meeting only to find out that they didn't participate or that the subject had nothing to do with their expertise. So make it a habit to reduce the number of attendees in your meeting so that it only involves those who actually need to attend your meeting.

3. Establish a clear agenda.

Since remote meetings are considered the least time-wasting option, you must ensure no one wastes their time attending them. Hence, you must establish a clear agenda in your remote meetings that covers what is going to be discussed during the meeting. You can see this with content creators when some of them explain what they are going to share in a specific video, blog post, podcast, etc. They have a clear agenda and stick to that plan so the audience benefits from it and feels like that they are not wasting their valuable time. Likewise, plan out a clear agenda step-by-step, explaining how many minutes everyone will spend chronologically on specific topics to have a meaningful and effective meeting.

4. Choose the perfect time.

Maybe you can't exactly choose the perfect time, but ideally, you will choose what works well for others. When scheduling a meeting, be sure to check in with others' schedules and calendars and see if they are available for it. A friendly gesture would be private messaging each individual to ask what time works for them. Then, you can set up a common time slot that works for everyone. This can be a challenge for dispersed teams when time zones can interfere with the exact planning; however, when you choose an ideal time and mention this in the invite, with every time zone converted for them, it makes things easier for your remote team.

5. Have everything prepared.

Since there are many video-conferencing tools and platforms you can use, ensure you choose the right one for your meetings. Furthermore, you must ensure that every one of your attendees has these tools available to them and is prepared. Otherwise, this can disrupt the meeting and will eventually cause some upset faces. Hence, before a meeting is scheduled, review all the tools in hand and make sure to have a concrete backup plan in place if your Plan A goes wrong. Always be prepared for any technical difficulties.

6. Provide a collaboration space.

If your remote meeting requires you to make use of collabora-tive tools to take notes or work on a project, make sure to mention this and link files in the meeting invites. Oftentimes, there will be instances when you ask your co-worker to take out their Google doc or presentation files, and this can drain a lot of time if they were not aware they needed them in the first place. Hence, mention and link collaborative spaces such as Google docs, spread-sheets, or design files and share with your attendees in advance so that they know what to bring.

7. Introduce everyone.

Good manners build a great personality. That earns respect from others. Hence, when starting a remote meeting, introduce everyone. This isn't always possible when your attendees list exceeds 30, but otherwise, it is essential to practice this to make everyone feel welcomed. After that, present your agenda when the meeting starts so that everyone knows what is expected from the meeting.

8. Engage people.

Be sure to give everyone a role in the meeting so that it becomes an all-round effective session and makes everyone feel a part of it. You can divide roles and assign someone to present a particular topic, one to moderate the session, one to take notes, and others to share their thoughts on the discussion. Basically, make sure everyone is doing something and is not left out of the meeting. You can think of creative ways to engage all the partici-pants by proposing a game or a fun activity to boost team collab-oration.

9. Always use an ice-breaker.

At times, participants may enter the meeting all stressed out and anxious about things. This is where using an ice-breaker can release all that tension and make all participants feel relaxed. This will also create a positive atmosphere in your remote meetings. Use ice-breakers at the start of the meeting to involve everyone; this can be simply asking everyone some informal questions and sharing a few jokes in the beginning to loosen all those nervous minds.

10. Follow up.

At some point during the meeting, you will be required to remind your attendees of what has been discussed so far and what will come up next. Essentially, keep following up with them regarding the crucial points covered in the meeting, as this helps them retain critical pieces of information and overall boosts the effectiveness of your meeting.

11. Use manners.

Maintaining some polite manners is essential to give everyone their respect and conduct a professional virtual meeting. One polite gesture is turning on your camera—especially when others have turned theirs on. It's never polite to be the only one not turning on your camera unless you have a good reason for doing so. When doing remote meetings, eye contact is important. Of course, when you stare at your webcam, that would mean that you are keeping constant eye contact with the participant. However, it is better to maintain eye contact with that person on your screen so you can study their body language, too.

Maintaining eye contact means ensuring you are not looking

down at your keyboard or having your eyes somewhere else on your laptop when you are actively engaging with someone. And lastly, it's good manners to mute your microphone when someone else is speaking. This can remove any background noises that could irritate the speaker. Moderate the chat in such a way that when one participant is giving a speech, everyone else's mics are muted so they can listen before sharing their thoughts.

12. Initiate action plans.

Finally, when the meeting is about to conclude, ensure you include action plans for your team or individual members. To get proper value from a meeting, there should be a call-to-action for your remote team to follow after it is over. This can include working on the upcoming or current project, or meeting a particular client. Raise your points and expectations in the meeting and conclude with an action plan. Furthermore, make sure to follow up with the progress by checking in with your participants to learn the status of the project.

Information to Put in a Virtual Meeting Invitation

When sending out remote meeting invites, you need to make sure that all relevant information is included in them so that your attendees will be prepared for the meeting and not left frustrated due to surprises. Of course, surprises can impress people, but they shouldn't be big ones that affect the entire meeting. Therefore, here are a few bits of details you should include in your virtual meeting invites every time. Include them in your notepad as a checklist before you send out invites to your remote team:

A concise subject line

Just a small and concise subject line that grabs the attendee's attention immediately. This includes mentioning the date, meeting name, and a few words to summarize what it is about.

Personal note

When sending a virtual meeting invitation, it is a great gesture to let them know who is sending that invitation. Be sure to add a quick note, such as: "Looking forward to meeting you regarding the software. Regards, Jane."

State requirements

If your virtual meeting requires you to bring some tools or resources such as presentations, reports, sketches, etc., then it is best to mention all these details along with the invite.

Date and time (include time zone, if necessary)

Without a doubt, include the meeting's date and time when sending your invite. Additionally, include the time zone to make it easier for dispersed teams to manage their schedules for the meeting.

Location or medium

Location should be mentioned if the meeting will take place in any physical environment. If it's a virtual meeting, provide the meeting link to the medium that will be used for the video conference.

Meeting objective

Make sure to include the purpose of this meeting and what outcome you are expecting to get from this particular virtual meeting.

Agenda

Lastly, include a detailed agenda mentioning all the topics that will be discussed during the virtual meeting. It is great to include any documents, links, reports, etc., to support the detailed agenda.

Effective Meeting Notes

The main goal of meetings is to take away key points and use them to fulfill an organizational task. This includes making it possible for your remote team to collectively gain insights and refer to them by themselves or as a collaborative unit. Therefore, you must make sure the notes taken down during meetings serve a purpose for everyone. A few ways in which you can take effective meeting notes is to first start with the basic information. So, that means always mentioning the date, time, and location first. Then, state the meeting objective in a concise manner so you are stating a purpose for this meeting.

Then, an efficient way to gather talking points and make them scannable for everyone is to filter them. Filtering down key points can be useful for those who attended the meeting and for those who didn't. Narrowing down points into scannable text makes it easier to share your points with any department. This makes comprehension better and saves time for everyone.

Furthermore, you can adopt transcribing whatever has been said in the meeting as another way of note taking. This makes sure everyone captures every crucial detail discussed in the meeting so they can refer to a written record to accomplish their tasks. However, it may require someone to transcribe who has good listening and typing skills to make sure everything from the recording turns into a proofread document.

BEST ONLINE MEETING TOOLS

What this chapter has taught you is that virtual meetings are one of the finest ways to communicate effectively with your remote team. Hence, video conferencing tools will help in that cause by truly maximizing your remote team's communication. There are many video conferencing tools out there, and so here are the seven most common ones you can start implementing as a default communication medium for your team.

1. Zoom

Since the lockdown in 2020, Zoom has exploded to be one of the most widely used video conferencing tools today. In the free version, you can add up to 100 participants in one meeting. On the flip side, free meetings end after only 40 minutes, so you will need to restart the meeting before that unless you go pro.

2. Skype Meet Now

Skype hasn't lost its touch since its early days, and with Skype Meet Now, it's offering some great video conferencing features in its free version. It offers unlimited meeting duration and can allow you to blur backgrounds. The downside is, you can only add up to 50 participants in the free version.

3. Google Hangouts

Google also offers a video conferencing platform that is extensively used by many around the world. It's free, simple to use, and fully integrated with other Google services like your Gmail and Google Calendar. However, you can only have up to 10 people in a meeting, and Hangouts is found to be limited on additional features.

4. Google Meet

For using more features that are not available on Google Hangouts, you can use Google Meet, which offers this service to G Suite for Business users. Its starting price is affordable at around $5 per month, and you can have up to 100 people in one meeting.

5. GoToMeeting

If you want to go for a more serious business video conferencing tool, then GoToMeeting is just that. Depending on the pricing plans, you can have between 150 and 3,000 attendees. It is quite business-oriented, making your meetings more professional. On the flip side, it doesn't come cheap.

6. Cisco Webex

Cisco Webex Meetings is a top-notch professional video conferencing tool, allowing you to hold meetings in HD. With its free version, you can add up to 100 people, and its biggest benefit is its unlimited meeting time. Unfortunately, this has been an overlooked gem of a tool because of well-known tools such as Zoom and Google Hangouts, which dominate the market for casual group chats.

7. Bluejeans

Lastly, Bluejeans is another video conferencing tool that is favorable for businesses. It is ideal for team collaboration meetings and has a unique Dolby feature that stands out against other video conferencing tools. The downside, however, is that there is no free version.

END OF CHAPTER REVIEW

- Remote meetings enhance communication, efficiency, saves time, reduces costs, and offers wider global reach.
- The five important types of remote meetings are one-on-ones, daily stand-ups, weekly meetings, retrospectives, and design sprints—with the latter two inspired by agile teams.
- The most common virtual meeting etiquette you must follow is defining the need, limiting the attendees, picking an ideal time for everyone, setting a clear agenda, having everything prepped, keeping every participant involved, and following up on action plans.
- In your virtual meeting invitations, always have a clear, concise subject line, personal note, meeting requirements, date, time, location, medium, meeting objective, and detailed agenda.
- The seven most popular video conferencing tools are Zoom, Google Hangouts/Meet, Skype Meet Now, GoToMeeting, Bluejeans, and Cisco Webex Meetings.

7

REMOTE MANAGEMENT

An effective manager is a role model to their team and helps them set the bar of performance higher by constantly reinventing themselves. Read on to find out how you, too, can be a successful remote manager, as this chapter focuses on the herculean task of managing a remote team and offers some useful strategies which managers can apply to effectively manage their remote teams.

MANAGING A REMOTE TEAM: A DIFFERENT BALL GAME

Without a doubt, the challenges of managing a remote team can be tough to manage compared to your traditional regime. In hybrid teams, maintaining the morale of employees itself can be challenging when a portion of your team works remotely while the others commute to the office daily. As a manager, you need to be prepared to build a solid work culture and manage these situations effectively. You are the conductor of an orchestra, and all you need to ensure is that there is a good flow in your remote team—minimize redundancies, establish a collaborative communication line, and continually support them with the right tools and technology. As a result, you will have an efficient group that you can manage—in most cases, on autopilot—and benefit from the labor and results your team produces.

CHALLENGES OF MANAGING A REMOTE TEAM

Regardless of that, problems do occur. Nothing is perfect, but this is when managers like you will need to weather the storm and successfully steady the ship. You are required to adopt unique solutions to several different challenges that may occur during your time as a remote manager. Let us refresh once again on some of the main challenges you can experience as a remote manager; in the next section, we will build on this to discuss the strategies to handle remote teams.

Lack of Real Interactions

Having a screen that divides you from your employees can mean there is a lack of interaction and supervision. Managers will doubt whether employees are performing their tasks, which is easier to supervise while in the office. In contrast, employees will feel a lack of interaction and support from their managers to successfully accomplish those tasks.

Unclear Expectations

While in-person interactions can result in employees being more clear on their goals, it doesn't necessarily mean that they will be 100% when working remotely. Without a doubt, making expectations clear remotely will take a bit more effort compared to when everyone is in the office. Hence, it is important to set expectations early on and to show direction when getting the message across.

Lack of Productivity

Although remote work is supposed to enhance productivity, some remote workers can't deal with working from home without proper guidance. Some of the reasons include having their family life affect their work schedule, having distractions all around, and a lack of guidance from their bosses. To combat this, it is essential to educate work-from-home employees on how to efficiently remove distractions and maximize their productivity when working remotely.

No Team Cohesiveness

Working remotely can easily result in an individual effort rather than working as a team under one roof. Therefore, using collaborative tools and a proper delegation plan are crucial to get everyone unified as a team. Moreover, managing both on-site and remote employees' needs can be challenging. When on-site employees find out that the remote team is receiving better treatment and benefits than them (and vice versa), this can affect the workforce's unity.

Social Isolation

Unfortunately, the remote work culture contributes to employees being socially isolated. This leads to loneliness, which can affect an individual's mental health and well-being. Furthermore, it gives employees a sense that they don't belong to the organization. To minimize isolation, always plan frequent casual remote meetings or real-life social gatherings to increase social engagement.

Lack of Accessible Information

Coming to the technical side of things, remote employees might often find it challenging to retrieve information and maximize their productivity. This could result from equipment problems, poor connectivity, lack of collaborative tools, poor data security, etc. Therefore, it is mandatory to educate remote employees with tutorials and a clear plan on how to use each tool to give clear direction for the technical work process.

STRATEGIES FOR MANAGERS TO HANDLE REMOTE TEAMS

When it comes to the virtual world, you will need to take some unique approaches. The challenges pertaining to communication, team coordination, and building a productive work culture can make managers lose sleep at night. However, here are a few strategies you can implement to handle your remote teams that will lead to improved performance from them.

Devise a Communication Manifesto

Lack of communication can result in low productivity and poor team coordination. Hence, you will need to devise a communication manifesto to set some expectations early on. A manifesto is simply a published declaration stating all the ground rules expected from a team. Your communication manifesto should include the communication channels that you will prioritize, the communication tool you will use for each channel, expectations of uninterrupted work, expected availability of employees online, etc. When you prepare a manifesto and present it to your remote team, everyone can get on board and adhere to the communication rules for effective coordination.

Pay Attention to Asynchronous Scheduling

Especially when it comes to managing dispersed teams, it is common that different locations and time zones can affect a team's morale and productivity if they adhere to a fixed traditional schedule. Therefore, allow flexibility in your team and enable them to work the number of hours they want. This allows your remote employees to manage their schedule and be more productive. To put this into full effect, make sure to get your point across effectively. Fix specific deadlines, collaboration guidelines, and other time management practices that employees can take into account so that your remote team can accomplish their goals within the desired time frame.

Have Virtual and In-Person Retreats

When you want to strengthen the foundation of your remote team, the best way is to improve the team's cohesiveness and togetherness. Hence, team-building activities are crucial to improve team engagement. One fine way to do this is by conducting virtual or in-person gatherings so that team members have the opportunity to learn more about each other and bond organically. Depending on whether your team is dispersed or co-located, you can organize a retreat however you like, as long as the main purpose is fulfilled—and that is to socially engage your team and bring togetherness into the camp.

Leverage Technology for Employee Productivity Tracking

It would be great to measure each employee's productivity for smooth project progress tracking and to make iterative decisions. However, it can be a challenge, especially when it comes to measuring accuracy. Therefore, implement project management software and productivity apps for employees so that everyone can stay on track with finishing projects on time and so you can keep up to date with each employee's overall performance. Having this insight can support you in managing your team better and making critical decisions at the right time.

Share Success Using Collaborative Platforms

You've got to celebrate the small successes that will breed a positive mentality and bring more results to your organization. In real life, employees celebrate by having a night out, grabbing a few drinks, having a cake party at the office, etc. On the other hand, when working remotely, this can be a difficult scenario. Hence why you must make use of collaboration platforms like Slack to your advantage. Create a separate channel on Slack that is dedicated to expressing your gratitude toward your remote team members' achievements. Giving employees the recognition they deserve will help with their confidence and motivate others to follow suit and aim for bigger things.

TACKLING BURNOUT

We can't manage remote teams consistently without talking about burnout. We are humans in the end, and we can push ourselves to a limit where we end up faltering. The misconception is that since employees and managers are in the comfort of their homes, they won't suffer from burnout. But this is not true, and you can suffer from burnout regardless of where you work. The common signs of burnout include feeling stress, anxiety, and loneliness.

Moreover, this gets worse when you feel tired all the time, don't find enjoyment in your job, are socially isolated, and, in some cases, are unable to prioritize your family life due to constant work pressure. These factors can result in demotivating you and eventually, no work can be done. Therefore, managers such as yourself must develop a healthy and positive work environment for your team to flourish in to minimize these burnout effects.

Tips for Handling Burnout

Here are a few essential tips you can incorporate into your remote team so that they can maintain a healthy work-life balance as well as their productivity in the long run:

1. Follow a routine.

A routine is definitely important to provide a plan to manage your time and energy, not to mention a direction. Allow employees to be flexible with their schedules and encourage each one of them to establish and maintain a healthy routine. Set time for their work sessions during the morning and/or afternoon. In addition, plan small breaks in between to get their minds off work by washing the dishes, cooking their meals, walking the dog, etc.

2. Prioritize meaningful things.

Much like your grocery list, there may be a lot of tasks you and your employees need to achieve but end up getting overwhelmed by them. This results in burning out. Therefore, ensure you and your team set priorities for the work by prioritizing the most important first, then attending to the least important ones last. One fine method you can use is implementing Eisenhower's Matrix into your work system. In Eisenhower's Matrix, you can prioritize work into four quadrants: most important/most urgent, least important/most urgent, most important/least urgent, and least important/least urgent. Based on the prioritization, you can know which tasks to do first and which ones to leave for last.

3. Maintain boundaries.

If working hard means that you will have to spend countless hours every night and sacrifice your sleep, then sorry, this ain't healthy. Simply put, this leads to poor health because you fail to set your boundaries and maintain a healthy work-life balance. At some point, you will need to be aware that if the work interferes with your personal life and personal well-being, then you need to maintain some distance from it and schedule the work for a more convenient time. Get this point across to your remote team so that they don't stress themselves out working and building unhealthy habits.

4. Take breaks.

Taking a break or having a rest is considered productive. No one should say otherwise. It is only when you overdo it that they end up calling you lazy. But you require rest in between work to recharge your batteries and go again. Incorporate a mixture of short and long breaks into your and your team's schedules. Short breaks include having a small stretching session, walking outside, reading, or having a nap. Long breaks include taking a mini-vacation or a sabbatical leave for a month.

5. Encourage social interaction.

When you think about all those tough times you go through while having a burnout, all you probably needed was a human being beside you, giving support and helping you unwind a little. Human interaction is key to how we maintain balance in this world. Therefore, encourage more social interaction among your team by having regular virtual meetings, or a gathering in real life. Consider this as a pillar to building a formidable and interactive workforce that will not burn out because they will never feel isolated or lonely.

6. Give priority to mental health.

Mental health is an important topic that mustn't be ignored. The result of burnout is an effect on the employee's mental health. Therefore, host webinars regularly to raise the importance of their mental health. Additionally, provide a few practices for how they can manage their stress and build a healthy work-life balance. Providing weekly mental health webinars will help your remote employees stay focused and provide them with a positive boost to work for the organization, as they know that you care for their well-being.

7. Use the right tools for work.

Sometimes, the burnout and frustration are because the technology keeps hindering their workflow and creating an unpleasant experience. Make sure to invest in the right tools for the right work purposes for your remote employees so that they can conveniently use it and achieve their tasks as a unit. In addition, provide tutorials or webinars on how to use these tools to maximize their efficiency and performance.

8. Train employees in emotional intelligence.

If your employees have high Emotional Intelligence (EQ), then they have the ability to manage their workflow well and minimize any symptoms of burnout. Having a good EQ helps in controlling your emotions and focusing all your energy in the positive direction. In a nutshell, every remote employee must be trained to develop a high EQ to withstand pressure and manage their workflow smoothly. Educate your employees by hosting webinars on emotional intelligence and providing them with the best practices to develop a strong mental state.

9. Always express gratitude.

There's nothing more sweet than a simple "well done" or a smile directed toward an employee for the efforts they have put in to accomplish a task. Always express gratitude to your remote employees so that they feel good about themselves and are more motivated to go further. You don't need to go overboard and host a party to show that appreciation. All it takes is small messages of gratitude expressed frequently toward your remote team.

10. Seek feedback.

One reason for employee burnout is a lack of freedom to speak up and share their thoughts. As humans, all we want to do is open up and share our opinions. Hence, you must provide a platform that is free for all to express that. One way to do this is by collecting feedback from your remote employees frequently on any matter. When you give each employee an opportunity to express their thoughts, it brings them out of their shell and brings a positive feeling to their mindset.

11. Establish trust.

When you establish trust and a sense of belonging in your camp, it leads to amazing things. It improves your team engagement, coordination, communication, and overall performance. You can build trust and togetherness by providing employee recognition, hosting virtual lunch or coffee breaks, delegating tasks or authority to employees, conducting team-building exercises, and promoting inclusiveness.

Lastly, never forget to monitor your risk of burning out. A good team doesn't exist if their leader ain't there. Thus, by using the above tips, make sure to treat yourself first to avoid any risk of burning out, and then promote these tips to your remote employees.

END OF CHAPTER REVIEW

- Some of the challenges that a remote team faces are lack of human interaction, unclear expectations, low productivity, lack of team cohesiveness, and being socially isolated.
- Devise a communication manifesto to have clear ground rules regarding the communication lines. Moreover, allow your remote employees to manage their schedules with flexibility to ensure they work productively and maintain a work-life balance.
- Host a virtual or in-person retreat and celebrate success on social platforms to boost employee engagement. In addition, leverage employee productivity tracking technology to ensure goals are being met.
- Some of the signs of remote employee burnout include stress, anxiety, lacking interest, being tired all the time, and being unable to prioritize family life over work.
- Maintain a routine, prioritize meaningful things, maintain boundaries, take necessary breaks, make time for socializing, emphasize mental health, and establish togetherness to minimize the burnout effects in your remote team.

8

VIRTUAL TEAM BUILDING

W hen everyone is in different locations and not hanging out by the water cooler, it's harder to form strong bonds and meaningful connections. Nonetheless, that doesn't mean it's impossible. A sign of a good team is their togetherness and the desire to fight for each other rather than satisfying their self-interests. Hence, you will need to build that team togetherness despite the challenge of working remotely.

This is a small chapter that is dedicated to learning all about virtual team building, why it is important, and how managers can forge strong relationships in remote teams.

IMPORTANCE OF VIRTUAL TEAM BUILDING

First and foremost, virtual team building is a set of procedures or activities that help form trust, relationships, and unify within a team to collectively achieve goals. Without a shadow of a doubt, to make remote employees more unified, managers should implement ways to bring them closer to each other and slowly build those bonds in the long run. Eventually, after effective virtual team building sessions, you will have a good team of people who are efficient and more motivated to bring results. And moreover, you will enjoy working as a team and being together.

Boosting Employee Morale

When remote employees are left alone to do their work, it promotes individualized effort rather than a collective effort. Therefore, with regular team meetings, interactions, and team-building activities, employees will feel more valued and understand how they function as a team. As a result, this helps in building a positive environment where mutual respect is formed, thus removing any team conflicts and disputes that can demoralize the camp.

Promoting Innovation of Thoughts

When talking about gaining a competitive advantage in a particular industry, innovation boosts those chances to stand out against the competition. For that, a team must foster innovation by brainstorming in groups, sharing opinions, feedback, and assessing every idea. Implement a strategy whereby your remote team is encouraged to participate and share innovative ideas with the team. In addition, promote constructive feedback and consider every innovative idea so that everyone feels valued and seen as a team.

Improving Work Collaboration

When you conduct virtual team-building exercises, it strengthens the work collaboration among your employees. It promotes team cohesiveness and as a result, takes their work productivity to another level. Having better coordination helps in saving their combined energy, saves time, and delivers quality in their work. Provide your employees with work-related drills that require them to collaborate better as a team to improve their work efficiency.

Building a Positive Work Culture

By interacting with people from different locations, time zones, and cultures, you will enable your team to build strong multicultural bonds that can boost a positive work environment. That is one great thing about having remote technology at your helm—you can bring people closer from a geographical standpoint. With many team-building exercises, regular interactions, and constant relationship building, you will make your remote team more versatile and bring a feel-good vibe to their remote workplace.

VIRTUAL TEAM-BUILDING EXERCISES

Since remote teams have fewer opportunities to socialize and build a strong bond, you will need to take advantage of times when they virtually meet up. By conducting some virtual team-building activities, it can help teams overcome barriers and develop team cohesiveness. Here are a few virtual team-building exercises, explained in brief, that you can utilize to improve your team's engagement:

1. Zoom or Microsoft Teams Background Challenge

Tell your team for the next virtual meeting to set up an innovative background from something that inspires them. This is a good way to learn about everyone's favorite movies, hobbies, and tastes. In addition, it is an opportunity to share a few laughs all around.

2. Lost at Sea

In this activity, you divide your employees into teams and provide them with a situation where they are stranded on an island and have to make use of the objects they have in their possession. This exercise helps in critical thinking and helps the group to collectively rank the most important objects in order. Moreover, dividing into teams makes it more competitive.

3. ABC Hunt

In this exercise, each participant gets a chance to draw up three random letters. Then other participants should grab three things that start with that letter from their surroundings. This makes the game challenging because there will be only up to 30 seconds given to participants to quickly grab things from their room that starts with that letter.

4. Escape Room

This is an exercise where employees collaborate to solve a series of puzzles that include word/math puzzles and codebreaking. If you want to test their critical decision-making skills in a team setup, then this is a fine exercise to implement.

5. 18 and Under

In this activity, employees will personally share a story or one thing they achieved before they turned 18. This exercise helps in breaking the ice and making everyone feel comfortable with each other.

6. Four Facts and a Fib

This is another informal exercise where each employee writes down five things or facts about themselves. The interesting part is that one of them will be a lie. Once everyone has written down those five facts, each person will take a turn to read out their five facts and leave it to the rest of the group to figure out the lie in that list.

7. The Baby Game

This is a hilarious game you can play by telling each employee to upload their baby pictures. You can assemble everyone's baby photos and present them over Slack or Zoom. Then, everyone takes turns figuring out who the baby photo belongs to.

8. Trivia

Conduct regular trivia competitions so that it keeps everyone engaged. You can organize it conveniently on Slack or another social media platform. This is a fun way to make your group more involved and entertained.

9. Blind Origami

In this activity, you will divide your employees into virtual pairs. Each one of them will have a sheet of paper to make an origami. Then, send one set of origami instructions to one person of the pair. They will try to instruct their partner (with their video camera off) to make an origami according to the set of instructions. The pair that makes the perfect origami wins.

10. Online Game Show

Similar to trivia, you can organize a reality show type of game show with all participants answering questions regarding general knowledge, pop culture, and many other topics. This is another fun game that helps to boost team engagement and also offers a good time.

DEVELOP AND DEEPEN RELATIONSHIPS WITHIN THE TEAM

As you know, relationships are formed organically when we meet in person. As for remote teams, you will need to replicate that real-life scenario virtually, and the good news is that it is possible. All it takes is a slight tweak and a bit of readjusting to the fact that they can still enjoy what life can offer together despite being distanced by screens.

A Virtual Space With No Bounds

Firstly, people need a platform to socialize with each other and make sure they form relationships. That is why social media has become part of our daily routines, because it fulfills that need. Especially when working with a dispersed team, you need to provide your remote team with a virtual space so that they can socialize frequently. That is why Slack will work best for you and other businesses, as it is an organized and collaborative platform. You can have separate channels for informal chat, a virtual water cooler, a book club, and many more. Slack can encourage both formal and informal communication styles, as talking only about work doesn't exactly improve those bonds. When employees exchange personal questions and share their feelings, you will see more bonds being created, and this is totally possible virtually. But remember that your socializing platform options don't end with Slack. You can incorporate Facebook groups, WhatsApp, and other social media platforms to keep your team connected and ensure everyone interacts with each other on a daily basis.

Have More Extracurricular Activities

A great way to engage your workforce constantly is promoting more extracurricular activities. Have different clubs such as a book club or a music club for those who share the same passion to meet up virtually on a regular basis. Transform your co-workers into friends when they meet up virtually and have a good time together. Organize a movie night where you provide everyone with a movie they haven't watched and you all watch it together while having your cameras and microphones on. For informal meetings, Google Hangouts would be the ideal choice for conducting them. In addition, if you want to make your employees healthier, encourage virtual fitness, where you all join an online workout program, take walks together with a camera on, share healthy recipes, and experience the progress together. As you can see, there are many ways in which you can conduct activities remotely to ensure your co-workers bond with each other well.

Take It Offline

Finally, why not take a break from the online world and go offline? If you are a co-located team, you can organize field trips where your team can go hiking or camping nearby. If you are a dispersed group, you can convince each individual to pick their adventure trip and have them meet virtually to share their experience with each other. For co-located teams, it is much easier to organize regular in-person meetings so that they can bond mutually. For dispersed teams, regardless of the fact that in-person meetings can be complicated to organize, you can still find joy in having that camera on during the virtual meeting and share your outdoor experiences with each other.

END OF CHAPTER REVIEW

- Virtual team building is a set of procedures or activities that help form trust, relationships, and unify within a team to collectively achieve goals.
- Conducting virtual team-building activities helps in boosting employee morale, promoting innovative thoughts, improving work collaboration, and building a positive work culture.
- Provide a virtual space for your remote team to socialize so that they can form bonds without any limitations.
- Regardless of being a remote team, you can incorporate extracurricular activities virtually to engage your employees and form a good mutual understanding.
- Feel free to take your meetings offline if you are a co-located team. If you are a dispersed team, you can still find joy in having that camera on during virtual meetings and sharing your outdoor experiences with each other.

9

HELPING EMPLOYEES GROW RESILIENT

E ffective management isn't limited to managers alone. Strengthening the workforce by helping them grow resilient and confident is one of the key ways to ensure a healthy work environment and a cumulative effort toward achieving common goals. That's how consistency keeps building and how good teams keep succeeding every time.

In this chapter, learn how managers can support mindfulness and resilience in their employees and nurture a healthy remote working environment.

MENTAL WELLNESS

When it comes to mindset, the remote work culture impacts a workforce's resilience in a different way. In the physical world, where you can embrace the shoulder of a fellow colleague when things aren't going well for you, it's not really the same when working remotely. You may reach for the phone to contact someone, but due to the delayed response nature and lack of human element in the communication, it simply doesn't feel like your problems are being solved. In a nutshell, it is simply essential to keep up with your remote team's mental health and well-being to ensure they are in full health and not letting the work get the better of their emotions.

Importance of Mental Wellness in a Workplace

The modern-day approach is to pick up on early warning signs before they unfold to a higher degree. The downside of remote work or working from home is that it has led to significant negative effects on an individual's well-being. Most managers have reported to have spent more working hours since the pandemic, which is quite astonishing because you would expect everyone to work harder in the office. Due to overworking hours, an employee can fall into a poor sleeping cycle and unhealthy habits. And can you believe the worst part? It's a silent killer, as no one will know who's suffering, though deep down, every individual would be open to seeking help in improving their mental health. Therefore, raising more awareness about mental health and wellness should be part of the organizational culture, and every workplace should employ mental wellness programs to help employees stay in a good frame of mind.

Mental Health's Effect on an Organization's ROI

As you have learned, the downsides of having poor mental health can lead to employee burnout and high stress levels. When employees exhibit more mindfulness, openness, and productive habits, it contributes to better productivity and active engagement, thus eliminating stress and the risk of burning out. It is essential to measure all employees' mental and emotional health, as they are the main driver to the company's productivity and endurance. With high productivity levels and consistent performance over a long duration, this manifests positive results for the team and the business. Moreover, it improves the team morale, and a positive feeling from one employee can spread contagiously among the entire workforce. However, the current situation tells otherwise within the U.S.: One in five adults suffer from mental illness, and these mental issues have been on the rise for the last 20 years. As a result, businesses lose up to billions each year due to employees suffering from mental illness. As you can see, this is huge and should be critically dealt with for proper functioning of the workforce.

Strategies for Improving Mental Wellness

Before mentioning some of the strategies, the first thing any manager should do is reflect on their willingness to be vulnerable and open up regarding any emotional and mental health issues they may have encountered. Do not normalize the topic and make it seem like a big deal. Your team needs a leader to take initiative and shed some light on the subject first. You take the lead, and others will follow suit.

Imitate healthy behaviors.

That brings us to the first point, and that is to be open to sharing your experience about any mental health issues you have encountered. Feel free to talk about any therapy or challenges you have faced with your team so that they will take this issue more seriously, like you do. In addition, it is in your best interest that you initiate self-care by sharing your experience and evaluating your mental wellness.

Keep checking in.

The significance of simply checking in with someone and asking how they are doing is huge. In fact, take it up a notch and go deep in your conversations. Ask what has been bothering them or if everything is going as planned. Establish a culture in your organization where everyone practices checking in on their peers and asking how they feel. Privacy does matter to your remote workers, but not to an extent that you end up alienating them. As a remote manager, one great thing you could do is include all your employees' birthdays and work anniversary dates on your calendar. This helps to remind you of all those important dates so you can wish your employees well privately or in the virtual space with other employees. As a result, it makes the group more connected and creates an open place to share anything that bothers them mentally.

Communicate more.

Employees who have been working with managers who seldom communicate with them are more likely to suffer from mental illness and other emotional issues. Maybe this can be the downfall for a laissez-faire leadership approach. You need to make sure to check in with your employees and communicate more regularly. This doesn't mean you need to micromanage them till you invade their privacy, but calculated check-ins and regular communication with your employees is crucial.

Be flexible.

Sometimes, your norms and policies need to be customized regularly to satisfy the employees' overall well-being and mental health. Hence, check in regularly with your employees and understand their feelings. Do not make assumptions or conclude that these issues will be a one-time phenomenon. In due course, many things can change in a working environment that can affect an employee's mental well-being. Therefore, be ready to offer flexibility and stay up to date with your workforce's mental wellness. Modify your policies wherever necessary to benefit your team.

Provide mental health-related programs.

One proactive approach is to stay ahead of the market and invest in training—especially when it comes to mental health and wellness. Firstly, it is essential to train managers to develop the skill of identifying early signs of mental illness in an employee and act early. Then, you can provide your workforce with mental health programs like EAPs (Employee Assistance Programs) and coaching on their emotional intelligence. Furthermore, you can act early and include mental health coverage as part of their health plan.

Measure actions.

Most importantly, measure the actions and issues faced now and in the past. Use it as an insight to learn and develop better mental health programs for your remote team. When you keep measuring and tracking the progress of your mental health regimes, it will give you more valuable insights and confirmation of whether the process is working or not. Do not leave things on auto-pilot and expect everything to get better.

MINDFULNESS

Mindfulness is the mental state achieved by actively practicing being aware of your current experiences and surroundings. It leads to deep thinking and a better psychological mindset. As a result, it allows individuals to show more composure and critically think about their life.

Mindfulness in a Workplace Matters

Undoubtedly, having mindfulness leads to better engagement on the job. Having your employees practice mindfulness meditation and yoga can lead to better focus, concentration, and positive involvement in the workforce. It improves their work experience, minimizes counterproductive habits, and gives them better job satisfaction. Mindfulness leads to that amazing ability to focus on tasks for a long duration of time and never worry about burning out. It is measurable that whoever practices mindfulness and expresses positive habits tends to excel at their job roles better than those who don't. Hence, it is imperative for employees to incorporate mindfulness into their daily routines for better work engagement and a positive work culture.

Ensure Mindfulness in Remote Work Culture

The positive work environment doesn't come without incorporating mindfulness regularly. Managers can play a part in raising this point and ensuring employees practice mindfulness in today's remote culture. Here are a few ways in which you can bring that:

Promote the helping culture.

This comes back to the point on how you should create a sense of belonging and togetherness in the team. When you establish that, employees are open to others, and this invites employees to help each other out. Normalize this culture of providing helping hands and checking in when an employee feels uncomfortable. But, do respect their boundaries as well.

Keep expressing gratitude.

There is a powerful science behind expressing your gratitude and saying "thank you." It brings a smile to the giver's face, builds self-esteem, and overall brings a positive feeling to the air. To generate more of that positive energy, keep practicing gratitude to your fellow employees and encourage this habit among your workforce. It is a great practice for someone to recognize one's effort and be thankful for their endeavors.

Learn to prioritize meaningful connections.

Crucially, look to prioritize family and friends first, since the remote work life can interfere with one's personal life. To make your work environment similar to a family, encourage employees to build better relationships with one another and keep making acquaintances. When you have a remote team that constantly looks out for each other, it creates a warm and friendly environment that anyone would adore belonging to.

Go outdoors more.

Inhaling that fresh air and looking at the nature around you benefits your mental well-being massively. It puts you in a relaxed and diffused mode of thinking—where you can brainstorm innovative ideas. In addition, having those regular walks outdoors will improve your physical condition and mood. Ensure you encourage your remote team to go outside regularly for walks, nights out, or to watch a movie; don't let the post-pandemic situation affect your decisions too much.

Tidy up.

When you remove the clutter or mess that has been lying around in your room or work table, you make your environment more organized and positive. Advise your team to tidy up their workspace and surroundings regularly so they enhance their focus and concentration levels significantly. It is proven that your environment plays a role in how productive and motivated you can be. Therefore, tweak your environment to your advantage.

MINDFUL RESILIENCE

Mindfulness resilience is the ability to cope with adversity by practicing mindfulness and experiencing a better and healthier mindset. With the pandemic and the rise of remote-based jobs, there is no denying that there have been more work hours put in by individuals, as well as unrest that leads to poor working conditions and unhealthy lifestyles.

Importance of Mindful Resilience in Remote Work Culture

With all these stress and hours put in by remote employees and managers, it has led to negative effects in work productivity and engagement. However, when an individual practices mindfulness and resilience together, they are developing a tough shell to withstand all unforeseeable challenges that may come their way. When your remote team practices resilience, they are prepared for the most uncomfortable of situations and circumstances. Life is challenging, and how employees can adapt and keep their composure shows their ability to work under pressure. Make sure to practice resilience early on to develop that characteristic in the long run and to succeed under adversity.

Benefits of Mindful Resilience

Indeed, mindful resilience offers numerous benefits that shape a remote employee's character and mental toughness. Here are a few major benefits you can get from mindful resilience:

Quality sleep

Lack of quality sleep leads to mental illness, disorders, and other health issues that have a negative effect on a remote employee's work productivity. However, mindful resilience calms your mind and removes all the toxicity, providing you with better quality sleep at night.

Stronger relationships

As mindful resilience removes all the stress and anxious thoughts from your mind, it paves the path to create better relationships with everyone you meet. You will find you have more enjoyment when conversing with people, as mindful resilience lets you feel more comfortable.

Better patience

Since mindful resilience helps in establishing more focus and concentration levels, you will find you have more patience when dealing with tasks and interacting with others. As a result, you will be less anxious about your surroundings and be more immersed in the moment.

Good problem-solver

A huge benefit of practicing mindful resilience is it can spark your creativity levels significantly. As a result of your better cognitive abilities, you will be seen as an efficient problem-solver for even the most complex of projects or situations.

Strategies to Forge Resilient Minds

Here are some strategies you can implement to promote mindful resilience in your workplace. Note that these steps can be taken by everyone, including you. So feel free to raise this advice to your team so they will receive positive effects in their mental health and well-being.

Meditate

Meditation is an excellent mindfulness practice, and it will help to boost your focus and concentration levels. When recommending mediation to your team, advise them to use meditation apps or calm background music that will help them transition themselves into a flow state.

Self-reflection

Self-reflection is a good practice for you and your team to implement in your lives. It encourages employees to be open and honest with each other by assessing their strengths and weaknesses. As a result, they can leverage their strengths significantly and try to find solutions for working on their weaknesses.

Practice journaling

Writing in a journal daily will help you and your employees to reflect on your lives and encourage self-awareness. It helps in transferring thoughts and feelings onto a piece of paper, thus making the heart feel lightweight and the mind more relaxed.

Set time limits

When you provide a time limit, you are providing employees with a practice to show urgency without getting too overwhelmed by the prospect of the time limits. It is a great way to combat fear and improve mental toughness.

Interact with like-minded people

The environment you're in plays a part in your mental health and overall feeling. Thus, try to spend more time with positive people who want to improve and cheer for you. Spending more time with like-minded people will help you and your employees gain valuable advice that can benefit you in the long run.

Exercise regularly

Last but not least, involve yourself in some physical activity. Exercise regularly, and you will see the numerous health benefits it provides. This reflects in your work and mental health as well. Advise employees to exercise frequently, and they will reap the mental benefits from all the endorphins released from their brains.

END OF CHAPTER REVIEW

- Strengthening the workforce by helping them grow resilient and confident is one of the key ways to ensure a healthy work environment and cumulative efforts toward achieving common goals.
- In a nutshell, it is simply essential to keep up with your remote team's mental health and well-being to ensure they are in full health and don't let their work get the better of their emotions.
- Imitate healthy behaviors, keep checking in on each other, offer flexibility with company policies, communicate more, invest in mental wellness programs, and measure actions to improve mental wellness among employees.
- Mindfulness is the mental state achieved by actively practicing being aware of your current experiences and surroundings. Promote a helping culture, express gratitude, go outside often, prioritize meaningful connections, and clear the clutter to maintain mindfulness in the current remote work culture.
- Mindfulness resilience is the ability to cope with adversity by practicing mindfulness and experiencing a better and healthier mindset. You can practice mindful resilience by meditating, exercising, journaling, self-reflecting, setting time limits, and interacting with like-minded people regularly.

10

THE REMOTE WORK ARSENAL

Without a doubt, modern challenges need modern solutions. And fortunately for you, this chapter has just that. This final chapter offers a glimpse into the necessary tools and software that modern remote managers must have to effectively manage their teams and boost productivity of their employees. Read on to discover a goldmine of helpful resources and tools for effective remote management.

ONLINE TOOLS/SOFTWARE

The pandemic has compelled organizations to disband their groups and retreat to their homes. But thanks to technology, employers, employees, clients, and many other stakeholders are able to connect with each other, thus maintaining normalcy. But many couldn't maintain the normalcy due to the technological implications and network complications. In this section, you will be provided with a few categories you will need to consider to equip your workforce with up-to-date technology. Moreover, under each category, you will learn about some tools you can start using straight away to improve work collaboration.

Online Collaboration

Firstly, organizations and teams require a way to collaborate daily. Thus, it is mandatory to adopt online collaborative tools so that remote employees share a common virtual space and can work together to achieve a common goal. Take the example of design teams. They consist of designers who optimize user experience for an app or software. Then, you have designers who work on the intricate designs and aesthetic looks. In addition, developers need to review the design plan and validate whether it can be developed. To accommodate a team of designers, their bosses, and many other stakeholders, there comes a need for a common collaborative tool. In such cases, they use mainly Figma and Sketch. This helps everyone to collaborate on the same dashboard in real-time.

Another great collaborative tool is to have a virtual whiteboard in your organization, because everyone comprehends better with visuals. Just like having whiteboards in the physical workplace, you can have virtual-based whiteboards and have your remote employees collaborate together to achieve their tasks. Utilize them for brainstorming, presenting strategies, and executing tasks for better team engagement.

Some of the top virtual whiteboard tools include:

- MURAL
- Stormboard
- Miro
- InVision
- Limnu

Instant Messaging

Written communication is vital in the business environment. Emails have been here for a long time and are still the most preferred way of formal communication in business. However, everyone has an email address and sends/receives many emails in a day. This is common, but what you should be equipped with is instant messaging apps due to the current remote work culture you have to get used to. To cater to a quick send-and-reply mechanism, messaging is a great way to have your team constantly connected with each other so they can develop a relationship faster than they would with emails. Instant messaging apps help with connecting teams living in different time zones and improve their collaboration significantly.

If you want a tool that helps you to build personal relationships with each individual just like in real life, then instant messaging is your virtual hero. Do keep in mind that you can incorporate business messaging apps like Slack and informal messaging apps like WhatsApp to have a balanced communication channel and be on a platform where most of your employees spend time. However, when it comes to business work processes, always communicate to your team the default platform everyone will use.

Some of the most common instant messaging apps include:

- Slack
- WhatsApp
- Facebook Workplace
- Microsoft Teams
- ProofHub

Video Conferencing

Moving away from written communication, you need that face-to-face time as much as possible to maintain that human contact despite the fact that it is done virtually. That is where video conferencing tools come to your aid. The thing you will love about video conferencing is the scalability, as you can have one-on-one meetings all the way up to hosting online workshops for hundreds of people worldwide. Businesses make use of remote meetings and workshops to try gaining a competitive advantage over their competitors. Despite the post-pandemic struggles and businesses looking to go back to physical meetings again, virtual meetings are still effective, and as long as you leverage the pros this medium has to offer, it will translate into your remote team's success. As you have learned in Chapter 6, as a host, you will need to follow some rules of etiquette to run effective meetings and maximize value from them.

Some of the best video conferencing tools were mentioned before in the Managing Remote Meetings Chapter; however, to refresh your memory, here are the tools you can use:

- Zoom
- Skype Meet Now
- Cisco Webex
- Google Hangouts
- GoToMeeting

Project Management

Having those workflows of projects moving through your business is a dream. Nonetheless, when it is not efficiently managed, it can lead to client dissatisfaction and loss in company reputation. In real life, project management can be handled with constant collaboration and meetings to organize work processes and accomplish those complex projects. On the other hand, it may seem complicated when done remotely. This doesn't have to be the case, because with many project management tools available online, you and your team can effectively manage your projects and use the power of technology and AI to support your business workflow. Some of the project management tools today make use of different techniques and methods, such as utilizing kanban boards, scrum, lean-agile work process, and many more. As a result, it helps organizations to keep track of business projects and ensure they accomplish each one within the desired deadline. Take the example of project management tools like Monday.com and Asana: You can have a birds-eye view on all your current projects with deadlines, and moreover set detailed work structures and assign duties or roles to specific employees. Adopting these types of tools in your remote team is massive and saves a lot of time and cost for your business.

Here are some of the most popular project management tools out there. Learn more about each project management tool and adopt the ideal one depending on the nature of your business:

- Asana
- Monday.com
- JIRA
- Trello
- Airtable

Online Documents

Indeed, your typical workflow is never complete without mentioning different types of online-based document apps to capture your written texts and numerical data. Whether you are a content-based team or you need document apps to write blog posts and marketing copy, you need an online content strategy. If you work for an accounting firm, you need to enter data and maintain bookkeeping online. It is crucial to utilize document apps because you can work on them offline, online, individually, or collectively.

Google Docs is one of the most used cloud-based word processors out there, with many companies working in offices or remotely incorporating it in their work routine. It allows users to efficiently share doc links, edit, suggest edits, and present as a view-only document to other stakeholders. When it comes to crunching those numbers and inputting important data, Google Sheets helps to maintain your essential records. It consists of spreadsheets, and, like Google Docs, you can share doc links and have your team collaborate on it in real-time. To work on projects and sort out other key areas in your business, it is mandatory to have these online docs.

Here are a few names of some cloud-based document apps your remote team could use:

- Google Docs (or Microsoft Word)
- Google Sheets (or Microsoft Excel)
- Quip
- Dropbox Paper
- Zoho Writer and Sheets

Sharing Files

All the inputting of data and preparing documents is good, but what's better is when you can share them with everyone on your team. In real life, all you need to do is pass the document from one hand to another. In the remote setup, you can do the same but simply pass the file from one computer to another. In social media, viral videos and photos spread instantly, and millions of users receive the content instantly. The same can be replicated in the business setting when remote employees can instantly share many files at once. Even if you require a presentation urgently delivered from your co-worker in China all the way to the U.S. within seconds, cloud-based sharing systems help remote teams accomplish their goals.

It is mandatory to have a cloud-based file sharing system as part of your remote work process to ensure a smooth workflow and maximize productivity from you and your team. So when you want to share those memos, ground rules, and important organizational structural changes instantly, make use of file sharing apps and their ability to store these files on the cloud over a long period of time. As a result, you and your team may not need to store any files in your desktops because everything is safely secured in the cloud.

Here are the best file storing and sharing apps that you must use for your remote business:

- Google Drive
- Microsoft OneDrive
- Dropbox
- WeTransfer
- Box

Other Specialties

Lastly, you will have to look at online tools that are used for a special cause. These specialized tools will help you in managing other key areas in your remote business. In one of the earlier points, you came to know about how design teams collaborate online. This leads to the point of product teams having specialized remote tools to design and manage their project files, eventually handing off the specifications to the developers. They require specialized tools that are iterative in nature so they can revisit and optimize their prototypes. With remote-based tools, this is possible.

Another scenario is scheduling appointments. When it comes to finding the best time slot available and receiving reminders, online meeting scheduling apps do a great job in bringing people from different time zones together to participate in that meeting. It allows each individual to sort out time slots in their calendars to see when they are available for a meeting. Once another individual books that available time, the meeting confirmation is sent to both parties. They both get reminders on the day of the meeting and eventually meet up virtually.

And another great initiative is to utilize remote tools that aid in your team's productivity and smooth workflow. There are many cloud-based productivity apps like Notion that give small teams transparency on what is happening in the workplace as well as details about every project. Then, you have smaller apps that make small tweaks to your working style. Some of these productivity tools out there can save you time by minimizing redundant work and maximizing your revenue. In a nutshell, ensure you use many specialized remote tools wherever you learn about them the first time and look to constantly improve your team's efficiency. Below, here are a few of the tools you can start using straightaway.

Some of the best design tools for product or creative teams:

- Figma
- Sketch
- InVision
- Whimsical
- Zeplin

Here, you have calendar and meeting scheduling-based apps that you can use to manage different time zones and streamline your communication process:

- Google Calendar
- Microsoft Outlook Calendar
- Calendly
- World Time Buddy
- Lucid Meetings

And here are a few productivity-based apps you and your team can use to hack your productivity system and be more efficient:

- Notion
- Evernote
- Confluence
- Flow Launcher
- F.lux

OTHER RESOURCES

Fundamentally, you will need to keep your eyes and ears open at all times and keep consuming information regularly. A remote manager must stay open-minded and learn information from many sources to stay ahead of the game and improve your knowledge intel. Indeed, your journey to learning the basics of managing a remote team doesn't stop here. You must keep consuming other resources to soak up new information and implement it in your remote workforce. Constantly keep reading or listening to information with regard to the remote work culture so that you keep getting inspiration to maintain an effective team remotely.

Read Blogs and Websites

There are many blogs out there that can help in providing you with management and leadership lessons. Moreover, there are websites that you can use to acquire remote workers and freelancers. Here are a few of the top choices that you should consider exploring:

Blogs

- **Escape the city:** A blog dedicated to the remote community that provides resources on managing a remote business.
- **Management 30:** A blog dedicated to leaders, helping them with leadership practices and maximizing their productivity.
- **Sorry, I was on mute:** A blog that dives deep into more about the remote work culture and encourages growing the remote-based tribe.
- **Home Business Magazine:** A blog that helps home-based entrepreneurs to flourish in their business and maintain a good work-life balance.
- **CoWorkaholic:** A fascinating blog that encourages traveling and working from anywhere, thus providing insightful value on that aspect.

Other Websites

- **The Write Life:** A website that brings remote freelancers and the passionate writing community together.
- **Nodesk:** A website that contains useful resources like blogs, books, newsletters, and connects organizations with remote employees.
- **Remoteworkhub:** A remote-based hub that has a job board and also plenty of insightful content for remote workers.

Listen to Podcasts

Whenever you are relaxing and taking breaks, listen to insightful podcasts. Traditionally, people listen to podcasts while commuting to and from work daily—making use of that time in their cars, buses, or the trains. But with more time on hand and in the comfort of your home, you can listen to content-rich podcasts out loud or in your cozy headphones.

These leadership and management-based podcasts come in different durations and styles. You can choose based on whose discussions and insights you find inspiring. And additionally, whose voice you find more soothing to listen to. Without further ado, I present to you a list of great podcast shows you should look into regularly. Try to listen to each one of them and feel free to pick your favorites:

- The LEADx Show
- Digital HR Leaders
- Accelerate!
- DriveThruHR
- Entrepreneurs on Fire
- The HR Happy Hour
- Ted Business
- What Great Bosses Knows
- Dare to Lead
- The Engaging Leader
- Beyond The To-Do List
- The $100 MBA
- The Shape of Work Podcast
- Vantage Fit Corporate Wellness Podcast
- The #AskGaryVee Show Podcast
- The 5 AM Miracle Podcast

Go Through Research Reports

When you go through and review many research reports, the proof is in the pudding. Ever since the 2020 pandemic, many have been intrigued about the remote culture and constantly kept assessing and testing various indicators regarding the remote workforce's productivity and efficiency. When you review these research papers and take away the key findings, you will learn more about how the remote work culture is slowly revolutionizing the way we work and conduct business for the future.

After studying these reports, you will have statistics to back up the claim that remote managers can leverage the positives of what remote work culture can offer and look to address the cons. Thus, you will be implementing a balancing act of producing positive outcomes versus minimizing the negative effects. Therefore, discover many research reports online and immerse yourself in the statistical proof of the remote work culture. Before devising any strategy and implementing it, you need to take some time off to do the research. As you know, preparation is key, and that is a sign of a great remote leader who is looking to guide their team to transition into a new working lifestyle.

END OF CHAPTER REVIEW

- Have these categories of remote or online tools sorted to bolster your arsenal for effective work productivity—online collaboration, instant messaging, video conferencing, documents, project management, sharing files, and other specialized tools for business and productivity.

- Read blogs frequently and utilize websites that encourage connecting employers with remote employees and freelancers.
- Listen to top-notch podcasts on leadership and management practices, thus gaining useful insights on managing your remote team.
- Go through and review research papers and reports to see the statistical proof. Leverage the pros of remote work culture and minimize the cons wherever possible.

CONCLUSION

The remote work culture is only the beginning, and it is here to stay. Your journey doesn't end here, but begins. This book was only the ignition to your desire to be an effective leader. That fire lies within every manager who wants to succeed in this new era. Hence why you have come all this way and successfully finished reading this book.

To summarize the important details, you have learned a lot:

- the present-age scenario, diving deep into knowing more about the remote work culture
- understanding the significance of establishing a remote work culture and creating a sustainable remote working model for your team
- the remote hiring process and how you can utilize the vast pool of talent by leveraging new-age technology
- all the important tips to welcome new hires onboard remotely and make them feel right at home instantly
- the importance of communication between employees and how you can maximize collaboration in a remote

work setting
- conducting effective remote meetings and maximizing value from having them frequently
- helpful strategies to manage your remote team and combat any challenges that await
- the significance of virtual team building and different ways you can implement to create togetherness and better work collaboration
- the importance of mental health and how you and your team can use mindfulness to stay resilient and maintain consistent productivity remotely
- finally, all the necessary tools and software you can use as your starter kit to seize remote management domination

Now, It's Your Turn to Lead

I hope my insights as a business coach and entrepreneur have brought you tremendous value in preparing you to be an effective remote team leader. Remote teams don't need managers, but true leaders who can support them constantly and look to battle challenges together. This book is a lesson that, despite what others say, you can make a difference in this new age, and all it takes is some discipline, heart, and critical decisions that lead to positive outcomes.

You now know how to be an efficient manager in the new work culture. Leverage your knowledge to empower your team! Be the new age manager by leveraging the right strategies and tools and set an example for others. If you have enjoyed reading this book and gained value from it, please do leave a review for wherever you got this book. I look forward to seeing you grow as an ultimate remote team leader.

REFERENCES

Anonymous. (N/A). *Virtual Team Building Exercises: Building Connections in Virtual Spaces*. MindTools. https://www.mindtools.com/pages/article/virtual-team-building-exercises.htm

Anonymous. (N/A). *How to Write a Remote Work from Home Policy | Remote Guide*. Wrike. https://www.wrike.com/remote-work-guide/work-from-home-policy/

Anonymous. (N/A). *What is Remote Work? A Complete Introduction | Remote Work Guide*. Wrike. https://www.wrike.com/remote-work-guide/what-is-remote-work/#what-is-a-remote-worker-and-how-do-people-work-remotely

Balkhi, S. (2022, February 3). *10 Ways to Make Your Remote Team Feel Connected*. Business.com. https://www.business.com/articles/remote-workers-feel-connected/

Birnir, A. (2022, May 24). *Find Remote Work Online in 2022 (Top 25+ Remote Job Sites)*. Skillcrush. https://skillcrush.com/blog/sites-finding-remote-work/

Biro, M. M. (2020, April 26). *8 Tips For Hiring Remote*. Forbes. https://www.forbes.com/sites/meghanbiro/2020/04/26/8-tips-for-hiring-remote/?sh=318e114c5de6

Citrin, J. M, DeRosa, D. (2021, May 10). *How to Set Up a Remote Employee for Success on Day One*. Harvard Business Review. https://hbr.org/2021/05/how-to-set-up-a-remote-employee-for-success-on-day-one

Sarma, S. (2021, December 1). *Top 15 Trending Podcasts For Managers*. Vantage Circle. https://blog.vantagecircle.com/podcasts-for-managers/

Savadmin. (2022, January 25). *10 Awesome Remote Work Blogs To Read In 2022*. Sorry, I Was On Mute. https://www.sorryonmute.com/awesome-remote-work-blogs/

Savina, A. (2020, March). *Remote Onboarding: How to Onboard Remote Employees | Miro*. Miro. https://miro.com/guides/remote-work/onboarding

Savina, A. (2020, March). *Remote Team Meetings Guide | Boost Meeting Efficiency*. Miro. https://miro.com/guides/remote-work/meetings

Savina, A. (2020, March). *The Remote Work Tools Every Team Needs | Miro*. Miro. https://miro.com/guides/remote-work/tools

Shekeryk, N. (2021, December 18). *How to Support Employee Mental Health in the Workplace*. Limeade. https://www.limeade.com/resources/blog/emotional-wellness-in-the-workplace/

ABOUT THE AUTHOR

Hollis Avery has been a business manager in about every setting you can imagine: Corporate and Not-for-Profit, as well as his own organizations. He found the management of remote employees to be different than anything he had experienced before and decided to add author to his resume. Hollis holds a bachelor's degree in Business Management and believes that every leader is just one amazing book away from being their best. This is that book.

For additional insights and resources on managing remote workers, you can find us at www.C3-publishing.com.

Printed in Great Britain
by Amazon

87352286R00088